T0193897

STORIES
TO TELL TO SHOW
HIS GREATNESS

God working through the highly educated

Eunice Anita

authorHOUSE®

AuthorHouse™ UK
1663 Liberty Drive
Bloomington, IN 47403 USA
www.authorhouse.co.uk
Phone: 0800.197.4150

*THE HOLY BIBLE, NEW INTERNATIONAL VERSION®, NIV® Copyright © 1973,
1978, 1984, 2011 by Biblica, Inc.® Used by permission. All rights reserved worldwide.*

Cover illustration by Dennet Offerman

Published by AuthorHouse 02/27/2015

ISBN: 978-1-5049-3717-7 (sc)
ISBN: 978-1-5049-3718-4 (e)

Library of Congress Control Number: 2015902077

Print information available on the last page.

CONTENTS

INTRODUCTION

Highly educated people have the tendency to believe that all they have achieved in their life is only because of their hard work. I have to admit that I used to think that way too. Of course you consider the effort your parent has made to help you, the fellow students who once helped and so on. I am not referring to the underdogs that people think of that with a lucky hand they made it. There is a lot written and filmed of those stories. I am referring to the middle and upper class family that supported their kids; send them to the best schools they could pay and so on.

The Organisation for Economic Co-operation and Development, shortly OECD, uses the classification of education level in accordance with the International Standard Classification of Education (ISCED) as the basis for her researches and publications on the education sector[1]. In accordance with the ISCED the education system has three general levels being the primary, secondary and the tertiary level. The tertiary level, which is split up in the three subsections type A, type B and advanced research qualifications, is described as the level that provides the necessary occupational, practical, technical or theoretical knowledge that is required for the professional to be able to function in the area chosen. The advanced research program has a focus on original research and advanced study.

So in short, highly educated people are those that have completed a tertiary education level. According to the OECD publication Education at a Glance 2014[2] was the percentage of highly educated people for the period under review and in the age category twenty five to sixty four, for the OECD countries equivalent to thirty three percent, twenty nine percent for the European Union countries and twenty seven percent for the G20 countries.

What do all these highly educated persons and I have in common? We were all taught during our studies that for everything in life there is an explanation in the natural. Whether it is an issue in the field of natural sciences, engineering, technology, health, medical science, agriculture or social science it can all be analyzed or explained by the several theories that we had learned. Tendencies like immigration or migration, inflation, devaluation of currencies, "El Niño" and "La Niña", and several other situations are analyzed by the natural. Do not get me wrong, there is nothing erroneous with all those analyses and explanations. The question is rather where did all of the wisdom of all the developers of all the theories come from? Where did your own wisdom come from? Maybe, inheritance of soft skills? If so, where did your parents or grandparents get their wisdom from? Have you considered all the knowledge and wisdom in your family as a blessing? Ever wondered what the purpose is of such a blessing within your family?

A lot of questions, isn't it? These questions and the answer to those questions are to lead you into the topic of this book, Adonai[A] working through the highly educated.

Adonai has been working through you and me, the highly educated ones, without you or me being aware of it. It may sound very silly as you read and reflect on these words, but that is the reality. Now that we are approaching the end times as is described in the bible in the book of Revelation, that revival was on the way and has arrived, Adonai is calling on his people to come out and proclaim His word. One time a fellow of mine asked me: "Do you believe in Jesus?" Upon my affirmative answer, he continued with the statement *"Well, that is unusual. Most people that I know with your level of knowledge and experience, do not believe in Jesus."* My response at that time was a simple *"Ah, it is their choice".* Later on I realized that I was wrong. It was not their choice, on the contrary, the time had not come yet for them to be activated for the kingdom of God. I was once part of the group that believed in a God that was only written in the

---

[A] Adonai: Hebrew name for the God of Israel

bible, but now I know that He is alive, and not simply alive actually alive and kicking among us.

Sadly enough a lot of families in the middle and upper class and not to forget the highly educated people, have forgotten the essence of life. They have forgotten Jesus.

In this book I want to illustrate the way the people in the middle and upper class live and think about life and based on some real life experiences I want to share with you why we, as highly educated people with roots in the middle and upper class society, should go back to Adonai, to Jesus whom had saved us too. You will read my story. What happened to me? How did my views on life change? How do I perceive the Almighty God nowadays?

I dedicate this book to Adonai, my Savior, my Healer, and my Deliverer as HE and only HE has inspired me to write this book. The plans and will are of Him and the experiences are mine. One thing that I know now for sure is that HE has created me for a purpose and send me to write this book for a reason.

May Adonai bless you all.

Eunice Anita

CHAPTER 1

The beginning

1.1 Introduction

Ever wondered why things happen in your life? Why everything seems to go wrong when you are trying at utmost to do what is right? Or everything is going well, however you still feel emptiness in your heart and your soul? You have the perfect family, perfect job and hobby, but still something is missing? I can tell you that those were some of the thoughts I had. At some point in my life there was a turning point. What happened to me, was not what I ever had expected or imagined. I was born in the late seventies and I grew up together with two brothers, my older sister, mother and father. I had, what many would call, the perfect childhood. No worries for food, clothing or transportation. All were arranged by my parents. My father had a good job and my mother took the decision to stop with her job to stay at home and look after her children. As a family, we had a lot of activities that we planned and executed together. We travelled regularly, so you would say nothing to worry about.

The way that God works cannot be analyzed or captured by our worldly ideas. He has his own way of operating. As human beings, we must accept this and give him the place that he and only he deserve in our lives. You may think now that this is an overreaction. I encourage you to continue reading. When you're done with this chapter, ask yourself if you still feel that the words in the introduction are due to an overreaction from my part.

1.2 The start

As indicated in the introduction I had a perfect childhood, what you could say like most highly educated. From my childhood, it was noted that I had leadership skills that had led to my appointment as child leader in scouting. On the other hand, at that time I was accused of being bossy and commanding by some adults. I have heard that so much that I decided to become more subtle and not interested in leading or taking charge. Now I know that children do show the qualities God has given them at a young age. It is up to the adults to guide them in the proper use of the gifts they have received from God. Unfortunately, as was in my case, adults have the tendency to stop the children from doing what they are good at, in the sense of behavior, instead of stimulating while giving guidance for appropriate habit.

Do you remember what you have thought yesterday on any particular subject or situation? Most probably your answer is yes. What if I ask you if you remember a thought from a year ago or from your childhood? Now that I'm walking on the path that God has put for me, I have started to look back at my life and my experiences from another perspective. I did not know that what you speak becomes life. In Scripture, specifically Proverbs 18 verse 21, it is clearly written: *"The tongue has the power of life and death, and those who love it will eat its fruit."*

I will illustrate you how true these words have been in my life. One thing I can assure you of and that is, that do not take for granted what a child says or think. When I was in the second grade at a certain point I was tired of waiting so long for the teacher to mention my name when she is passing through the attendance list that is sorted on last name. I thought one day, when I marry it will be with a guy whom last name does start with an A. This way, my children will not have to wait that long for their turn in the classroom. Do I remember any other specific inspiration that I might have had from that period in my life or as a teenager? NO. This is the only and I emphasize the only thoughts that I have had that

I remember from my childhood and teenage years. The funny part is that around my eighteenth birthday, this thought had passed through my mind. I laughed at myself kind of saying, what a wish for a girl of seven. Years later I got married and some years after I had my first child, a beautiful daughter. One day while filling a registration form for my daughter, the idea of the seven year old girl came to my mind and then, just then I realized that the thoughts of a child could be more than just feelings. You guessed it right, the last name of my husband starts with an A, meaning that my children will always be in the upper section of a classroom attendance list sorted by last name.

I want to go back with you to my education as it will turn out later that the path I have walked was the path God had chosen for me. My school career went on without major problems. At the high school I had some problems with language lessons as I was not much interested in all the technicalities like punctuations, accents, etc. Later on when I realized that those lessons are needed in order to graduate, I changed my mind. My favorites were accounting, economics and mathematics what has lead me to choose to study Accounting and later on Auditing. As a student, I combined my studies with some extracurricular activities at the university what brought me knowledge and skills in several areas. Little did I know at that time that all those knowledge and skills would be of great use for the ministry(ies) where God would send me to assist. After finalizing my bachelor studies, I started to work at a Big-5, nowadays a Big-4, audit firm[B]. Later on while working I achieved my Master degree. Up to this point life was as many would say normal. Before I continue, it is necessary to give you a picture of my spiritual life up to that point in my life.

On the spiritual level I grow up in a family bound to the Catholic Church. The primary school also was associated with the Catholic Church and provided several teachings and songs on biblical topics. My

---

[B] Big-5 audit firm was a reference used in the late 1990's for the audit and consulting firms Arthur Anderson, Deloitte & Touch, Ernst & Young (E&Y), KPMG, and Price Waterhouse Coopers (PWC). After the split up and sale of Arthur Anderson audit practices in 2002, the group is referred to as the Big-4 audit and consulting firms.

family attended on a regular basis the Sunday morning services at the Church and sometimes even the seven o'clock service on Sunday. I have to admit that I was not always happy on this fact, but what can you do as a teenager. Believe in God the Father, Jesus and in mother, Maria as is the practice in the Catholic Church, was common in the family. All was good in all sense of life till the moment that my father passed away in a tragic way. My family is left behind with questions that we believed will never be answered. Now that I am writing this book I have been able to put all that had happened into perspective. This may sound awkward to you, so let me tell you how I received this revelation. A couple of days ago I heard the testimony of the servant of God Ruben Hernandez, author of the book *"Herido pero aun Caminando"*[3], who explained that he has lost his daughter in a tragic way while he has been a servant of God for years. He had gained many souls for God, but still had lost his daughter. He had asked himself how he will be able to tell his soul to not forsake God after the tragedy; how to continue gaining souls for God. He said despite all, he knew that God had not left him. He knew that a price had to be paid to follow God and this was his price. This testimony made an impact on me. I kept thinking about the way the servant had said how to tell his soul to continue trusting God. Suddenly, I went back with my thoughts to the tragedy within my family and I realized that, that was the price we had to pay. Why? The answer is simple. The almighty God is calling my mother, my sister, my brothers and me to serve him in spirit and in truth. I have to say that it took years for us to realize this. First, we had to deal with the tragedy. You might be thinking now that a tragedy must or will happen to you or a loved one, do not worry for you can shake that idea off. Have you considered someone in your family, you could go generations back, whom had already paid the price for your family? Please do not mistake the price paid by Jesus at the cross and the price to be paid to follow Jesus for Jesus had said to his disciples to leave everything behind and to follow him (Matthew 4: 18-22). The price to follow Jesus nowadays might be leaving behind what you have always known and/or is attached to for moving to another country or Continent in order to work as missionary, for example. It is also possible that the price that you have to pay is related to quit something that you are used to do or simply taking care of your fellow citizen, open your house as shelter for others or provide help, financially or non-financially. Only God knows from whom and how He is to request a price to follow Him. One thing God has promised us for free and that is His presence that leads to deliverance of sickness and evil spirit, joy, peace and all that another human person cannot provide. All of this was unknown to me and my family at an earlier point in our lives.

My mother a strong woman of faith, encouraged us, her children, to trust God that all would be well despite the situation we were in. It is in these kind of situations that you notice how deep your faith in God is and whom really cares about you. In the first days there are a lot of attention and help however after the funeral, everybody goes back to their normal lives and you are left with your <u>new</u> situation. It was hard, very hard, but all we as family were able to see was the grace of God. Though the main breadwinner was gone, we had no financial need or other basic needs. People who have approached my mother, my sister and me in the later months told us that we look good. We took a look at each other and asked ourselves why is there the expectation that while going through such an experience all that you can do is be pissed at life and at God? Are we that different that we have not been sitting in a corner just to mourn for days, weeks, months and years? The mission of this book is not to elaborate on the situation when a family member is gone, but it is worth mentioning that, it is never easy. As family more than ever we have put our trust in God, not knowing that what happened was the beginning of the road on which God would call us, each one of us, to serve in His house.

In order to understand the developments in my spiritual life, it is necessary to understand the process my mother went through as she is the first one out of the family that God called and she obeyed. Why I am saying that she obeyed I will be explaining in the next chapter. My mother was several years active in a prayer group that had meetings every Monday morning. It was for her one of the moments to speak about God and pray to God. The prayer group was bound to the Catholic Church. After the loss of my father, my mother continued to attend the meetings of the prayer group. A year and a half later, I got married and left my parents' house to start a life with my husband as a couple in The Netherlands what is approximately nine thousand miles from my birthplace. We married in late December two thousand and three and in January two thousand and four, we took the plane to The Netherlands. It was bye, bye, summer and hallo winter; oh what a cold. In the meanwhile, my mother started to adjust at her life with her daughter living so far away. Due to the technology of this decade, we stayed in close contact with each other while being attentive to the time zone differences. The months went by and the year had changed. At some point in time, a cousin of my mother tells her of a Pastor that has a program every morning at a local radio station. The Pastor is a new Pastor that just started with a (new) Apostolic Prophetic Church. Her cousin tells her that the way this Pastor explains the gospel is different and that does inspire her. My mother, who has gotten the information, makes the decision not to do anything with it. Later on, due to a difficult situation mother encounter, not caused by her, but by an acquainted, she takes the decision to attend a service of the Pastor her cousin had told her a long time ago about. She went to the service together with the acquaintance, not knowing that God is calling her not her acquaintance. The experience is one she will never forget. This is the start of the family moving into the path that God had prepared.

Several years later, my mother tells me that now she understands the words that were spoken to her in the early 1980's. The charismatic season, which was in the seventies was experienced by a lot of people known by my mother. When I was about three years old, a lady whom was very active in the charismatic movement in the time that the Holy Spirit had been manifesting in that movement had told my mother that she is seeing my mother walking with three children towards Jesus. My mother at that time happy married with one child, considered that as a loose remark because she was not yet thinking of having more children and she found it very strange that her husband was not mentioned as part of the group walking towards Jesus. About thirty years later, my mother was a widow with three children, working on her spiritual life and her children had become aware of the special calling God had put on their lives. The loose remark of back then is now so real that cannot be doubt about it. Once more we realized that the way God operates cannot be rationalized by our human minds. This is not the end of our walk on the path God has designed; I assure you that as it turns out this is only the beginning.

Let me go back to when I started to walk on the path. I was living with my husband in The Netherlands and working at an audit firm having nothing to worry about. We had travelled around Europe, expanding our horizon and knowledge of cultures. Soon our family grows and a beautiful daughter and a handsome son are welcomed. At a certain point I started to feel the emptiness in my heart. When I looked around me, nothing is missing, still I had the feeling that something is missing. I neglected that feeling and continued with the here and the now until I realized that situations do not happen by chance. Up to that moment, I had looked at life situations like circumstances that happened by chance. Little did I know that God was paving the path, which He had already designed for me.

One day my brother called me to inform me that there is a vacancy at my former employer on the island of Curaçao. We talked about, but I told him sadly enough, the family is not ready to move. A couple of weeks later he calls me that the vacancy for manager Audit had been fulfilled and we agreed that it was indeed not yet the time. Three weeks had passed by and we received the information that my mother in law got sick. When you have children and all of them live far away, it is not easy for either party. While thinking what could be done, who could go to the island, I got a phone call from my brother that the function became vacant again as the hiring of the prospect candidate did not go through thinking that it is kind of a perfect moment to move and live closer to families, I applied for the job after consulting with my husband. I believed that God has given me a chance after all to be on the island and the timing is good as we will be able to be closer to my mother in law. The agreement with my husband was that I would move on short notice with the children while he would search for a job on the island and sell our house in The Netherlands so he can come over for us to be together again. With the expectation that in about a maximum of six months the job for my husband or sale of the house would be accomplished, I started a new chapter in my life. Later on it would turn out that the plans of God are totally opposite to what I had assumed for the Words spoken in 1 Corinthians 7:5 would become true in our life. 1 Corinthians 7:5 says *"Do not deprive each other except perhaps by mutual consent and for a time, so that you may devote yourselves to prayer. Then come together again so that Satan will not tempt you because of your lack of self-control.*" At the end my return to the island was meant for God to start working visibly in my life and to send me back for His work in The Netherlands. I am grateful for the fact that my children had the opportunity to live some years nearby their grandparents what had a very positive effect on the health of the grandparents because they now had to throw balls, play games and read books for the grandchildren, isn't that wonderful?

To be honest, when looking back all the elements that God was working in my life were present nevertheless I was not aware of that. The opportunity for a job in my place of birth came to my attention and my mother in law becomes sick for a short period in the same timeframe. Coincidence?

1.3 The names of our children

Before continuing with the story, I want to go back with you to a period where God was already paving the pads for me still I was totally not aware of it.

My parents gave me the name Eunice. In nineteen ninety six we were as a family on a trip to the beautiful island of Puerto Rico in the Caribbean. There we had seen a store that was selling several items, displaying names and their meaning. We found it fun and I had asked my parents if I may buy an article with my name and meaning on it. After some searching, I got approval of the purchase of a keychain. I still have the keychain and from time to time I read the text written on it. The name Eunice[4] has a Greek origin and according to the information the shop had it stands for victory and a character that does not avoid obstacles but rather enjoys reaching the unreachable. On itself a self-boosting text that when you are in your teenage years you look at it with other eyes than when you are in the thirties. I'm spending some time on the explanation of my name as it will turn out later that the link with the bible has always been as clear as water but we were never aware of it. The text of 2 Timothy 1:5 will become reality in my life in a way that I could have never imagined.

When I was pregnant with my first child, I did the prescreening of names by searching the internet and books for the meaning and relationships with events that were coupled with the names. My husband and I wrote a list of names that we considered appropriate to give a child, so we agreed that when she is born, we will decide which name it will be and we did. When we had her in our arms and we went through the list of names, we both had the feeling that she did look like a Tiffany. When I got pregnant with my second child, we used the same procedure. When our son was born and we went through the list of names, I indicated my preference but my husband still had some doubts. We were at the hospital, a couple of hours after the birth of our son. I was in the hospital bed recovering from the hard work and my husband was sitting in the chair next to my bed with the list containing the prescreened names. He read from the top to the bottom and from the bottom to the top. He took some minutes to think before he looked up to me and said: "We shall name him Timothy for he will then have the same initials as his sister. When letters arrive at home addressed to T. Anita, we shall give them all to Timothy. If one of those letters turns out to be a love letter to the sister, he does know about it and he shall teach the sender that no one messes with his sister." I looked up at him and I had to smile before I could reply that actually that is what my parents should have done with him, after all I have two brothers whom could have done the job. He looked at me and had a big smile on his face. To us, that was the reason why we named our son Timothy. We had laughed weeks about this and to everyone whom had asked in the first days why the choice, that was the story to tell. When my son was about two months old, my mother had decided to look up the stories in the Bible in the book of 1 Timothy and 2 Timothy for she had wanted to know the story of Timothy as written in the bible better. At that time she was at our house in The Netherlands. When she had read the text of 2 Timothy 1:5, she stopped reading and called me in order to ask me if I knew that according to the text Timothy is the son of Eunice. The text of 2 Timothy 1:5 says "*I am reminded of your sincere faith, which first lived in your grandmother Lois and in your mother Eunice and, I am persuaded, now lives in you also.*" To be honest, I did not know and my husband for sure had no idea. I told her that and I told her again of the reason why my husband had decided to give the baby boy the name Timothy. At that time we were amazed by the coincidence, now we know that God works in different ways.

1.4 The Diamond

Diamond, the gem that people have given more value on this world. Diamond Source of Virginia, Inc. describes on her website what is a diamond, what it is made of and the diamond cutting process[5]. The diamond cutting process is described as follows: "*A newly mined rough diamond looks more like a piece of glass washed up on a beach than like the polished loose diamonds and diamond rings sold in jewelry stores. Bringing out their beauty requires the skill and art of a trained diamond cutter. While incredibly precise, computerized machinery is now used in some parts of the cutting process for some diamonds, most of the work is still performed by hand using meticulous techniques passed down over the generations*"[6]. The essence of the process is that a raw material is cut and shaped in order to become a sparkling, valuable piece. You might be wondering why I'm telling you about diamonds and what the link is with my spiritual life. Before I tell you the connection with my spiritual life, I want you to pay attention to the diamond cutting process in relation to the way God works. The Word of God tells us in 1 Corinthians 7:20 "*Each person should remain in the situation they were in when God called them*". These words are repeated in verse 24, so it is very important. When I related this verse with the diamond cutting process, I realized that indeed God is calling me to come to him as content, happy, silent, dirty, dishonest and unhappy or in whatever situation I was. He will mold me, cut me spiritually and shape me spiritually in order for all the good He has put in me can shine. So far it sounded nice and looked nice till I realized what the cut, mold and shape represented in my life. I can surely affirm that I was cut, mold and shaped, nonetheless throughout all this trial, God was by my side or was even walking in front of me. He had never led me alone. For you to understand, and be able to relate back to your personal situations, I will be telling you about my walk with God.

As I have indicated in the previous chapter, I moved early two thousand and ten together with my children to my place of birth with the expectation that my husband would follow soon. Despite the economic crises and the fact that sale of houses was at a low point in The Netherlands, I kept the positivity that we would be able to sell the house. The alternative plan was to rent the house, if my husband found a job at our place of birth. The days passed and no change in the situation. The days became weeks and the weeks became months. I was still optimistic that all would be well. In the meanwhile, my mother invited me to go to the church services with her. I, in turn, responded that I did not consider it necessary. I was happy for her that she has found new strength through the new church, but for me, I would continue to visit the Catholic Church. My mother respected my point of view and so she went to her services every week while I visited services when possible, let us say when I was not busy working overtime. The turning point in my life came in the month of May. As May is the month in which my mother celebrates her birthday and Mothers 'Day is celebrated almost worldwide, I decided to join my mother on Mothers 'Day to her church service. I thought it was my decision, now I can say, it was God's decision.

We arrived at the service of the church, which back then was known as *Iglesia Lluvias de Bendicion Curaçao* and we were welcomed by the people present. In chapter 4 I will explain the current name that the congregation has. I have to say that a few people were already familiar to me as they used to visit my mother at home. Upon arrival you feel a warm atmosphere, the care and love among the people was evident. The service started soon after we had arrived. The service would be led by Apostle Orlando Balentina and Prophet Xiomara Balentina[C]. The musicians started to play and the music was flowing through the building. At a certain point I felt a strange feeling inside of me, even so I said to

---

[C] Apostle Orlando Balentina and Prophet Xiomara Balentina were ordained in November 2006 by the servant of God Apostle John Eckhardt of John Eckhardt Ministries, founder of the IMPACT Network and the Apostolic Institute of Ministry (AIM).

myself, do not exaggerate, nothing is happening. The Apostle started talking to the public while walking around. I could not understand what I was seeing around me. A person upfront at my left hand started to scream, another was making strange movements, and then again another was touched by the Apostle and went down. I was looking and found it so strange. Suddenly, the Apostle stopped in front of me, took a look at me and said *"You think you are smart"*. After speaking, those words, he continued walking around the room. I was left with a lot of questions in my mind: What is this? Why did he say that? Why me? I'm smart, am I not? I mean, I completed a Master study? Does he do that with all first timers? I have to say that the questions continued to pop-up in my mind. A funny part is that right after the action of the Pastor, I turned to my mother with the look of *what is this* but I had not spoken a word. All she did was to smile at me. I think, I kind of missed a part of the service due to all the questions that were popping up in my mind. For my feeling that day, the service was very long, but finally it ended and we headed home. The moment we entered the car, I looked at my mother and asked her what had happen inside. She came up with a kind of sales story, by saying not to take it personally, to look at it as a new experience and so on. Of course, she was trying to make me feel comfortable, something I surely was not at that moment. I have to say that despite the statement the Pastor, I was still intrigued by the strange feeling inside of me. Curious and intrigued as I was, I decided that I would go another time again just to see if the things I have seen and experience the first time happen again, however not now. It took a week or three or five for me to get in peace with the statement made by the Pastor. In the meanwhile, I did not go to the service. Four weeks after my first visit to the service, the Apostle passed by at my mother to leave his children for babysitting. That week he came twice, to leave the children at my mother's; something that does not happen often. On both days, he had asked my mother for me. The first day, when my mother had told me that the Apostle had asked for me, I reacted very chilly. On the second day, when my mother told me the Apostle was present, I decided to walk towards him to greet him. That is polite, isn't it? We greeted each other and talked shortly. Then he asked me to join the prayer group on Sunday morning at 5 a.m. This group reunites every Sunday morning to pray for the main service that would start around 10 am. My first thought was 5 a.m. on the Sunday? It must be a joke. To be polite, I said that I would think about it. He was happy with that answer and I was happy because after all I did not say yes. I went back inside the house and later on I told my mother what the Apostle had asked me. She asked me if I would go and I had said that I would think about. My brother, whom has always been keen on making jokes and a little bit of teasing, started to ask me, since the moment he heard of what had happened while he was not at home, everyday if I would go to the prayer group. We were making jokes about it and Saturday evening was the icing on the cake. He kept asking me every ten minutes Are you going, are going tomorrow? Then he had changed it to the statement "*Tomorrow, oh tomorrow is the big day.*" That was annoying, but I was able to keep my patience and not go into the provocation. You might be thinking that it was easy for me to make jokes together with my brother about the church and the prayer team. Deep inside of me God had been working for a while already. At that moment my children and I had been living about six months separated from my husband. My patience with the situation and the hope for my dream to have a united family started to shatter. As I had already lost the perfect family, what could I lose by going to the prayer at 5 in the morning? With that in my mind, I told my mother that I would go when she asked me just before going to sleep. Waking up early is not my best friend, except that Sunday I was awake around ten passed four in the morning and prepared to leave for the prayer session. My mother had set her time clock for 4.15, yet found me awake when she had woken up. She called the Apostle 15 minutes later to remind him to pick me up. We called three times, but sadly enough we could not reach him. At last my mother decided to call the Pastor, Pastor Renny, as she explained to me that he leads the prayer group for men that reunites nearby my mother's house. So actually, every Sunday morning there are two prayer sessions. Initially I wondered, joining the man prayer team? On a second thought, as I am in need of prayer for my husband, for him to get a job on the island, joining the man prayer team as representative of my husband did seem as an excellent idea. My mother reached the Pastor on the phone and explained the situation to him and he then said that it would be fine for me to join the group, so I took my mother's car and went to the prayer session. Later on I would get to know through my mother that when the Pastor had seen me arrive at the prayer location, he separated himself from the group to ask God what he is supposed to tell me. He told my mother when the service of that day had finished, that in the morning he had received on his heart to tell me that when I'm home, to go into my room and pray to God and God himself shall answer me. To be honest, I cannot recall exactly what the Pastor had told me that morning. What I do remember is that the essence of his saying was that my questions would be answered. At that moment, those words uplifted me. The Pastor finalized by motivating me to attend the main service later that morning. I went home with the feeling that I have to go to the service. I arrived home and my mother, as she told me later, consciously did not ask me what had happened at the prayer session. She noticed that when she was preparing for service, I started to prepare my children too for leaving home. She thought that something had happened, but still did not ask. While we were preparing for the service, it suddenly started to rain. Not a light, a short rain cloud passing by, on the contrary it was a heavy rainfall that was accompanied with lots of wind. As suddenly as it started, it stopped. That day the service had to take place in a building that was semi-opened, consequently due to the rainfall, the place was partially under water. Knowing that, my mother said that she would take some materials to help clean up the building and therefore she had to leave earlier. Therefore, my mother went to the service site without us. Later on I went to the service with my children and what a service it would turn out to be.

1.5 Attending a second service

That day I went to the prayer session in the early morning hours and later on to the main service, the second time that I would attend the main service. Well, there is one thing I can tell you about that day, my activation for the work of God took place on that day. When we had arrived at the service, the worship was already ongoing and I was just in time to let my son, of eleven months, go with the bus to the location where the children's service would take place. My daughter did not want to go with the children and as she was so upset, she stayed with me at the main service. Later on my brother, whom had been teasing me at home, would join us at the service and have a seat next to me. That day there were about two hundred people present. We were sitting in the first part of the last section on the right hand in the room. The service went on and some of the stuff I had seen on my first attendance happened in this service. That Sunday, we had planned at home that as soon as the service would be over, we would leave in order to attend the birthday party of a niece whom just had turned five. The Pastor was busy in the front praying for a person when I had decided to leave as my daughter had fallen asleep in my arms. The service was almost reaching the end so I turned to my brother and told him for letting us go and we would ask my mother to wait for my son as the children arrive. Suddenly I heard the Pastor say in the microphone *"whom is talking about leaving?"* He started to walk straight to me by asking the persons sitting in the rows in front of me, to make a path for him by removing the seats. My brother and I looked at each other as we were astonished by the side path that the service was heading to. The way we had spoken to each other, a person sitting two rows in front of us could not have heard us. How is it possible that the Apostle knows that we were talking about leaving? The Apostle continued by putting the microphone in front of my brother's face and asking him what I had told him. When my brother answered, the Apostle told the audience, that the Holy Spirit knows everything and that the Holy Spirit had guided him to me. The Apostle took my daughter from me and she woke up immediately in his arms. She did not cry, scream or react as children are used to do when they just got awake and realize that they are not with the person(s) they are familiar with. Instead, she laid her head down on the shoulder of the Apostle like he is her father. Then the Apostle instructed me to follow him to the front of the room where he handed over my daughter to his wife. Amazingly, my daughter did not protest. Then the Apostle turned to me and told me that today is my day of change, that after this day, nothing will be the same. He told me that the answer I was looking for that God and only God would give it to me and for that I would have to go into my room, kneel down and ask my questions to God. All I could feel when I was standing up front was an urge to cry. Cry for my situation, cry for the fact that I was standing in the front while I did not want to; cry, cry and cry. I was not aware that someone else was also crying at that moment. The Pastor, whom had told me in the morning that God would answer me, was crying as for him the words the Apostle had spoken to me were the same words he had received to tell me in the early morning hours. To him God was real, but up to that moment he had not experienced that the word he had received in the morning to be repeated by the Apostle on the same day just a couple of hours later. My experience was a revelation, or better said, another revelation of the greatness of God for a man of God.

While the Apostle was praying, he lifted his hand, stretched it out to me and touched me on top of my head. The next thing I know is that when I opened my eyes, I was lying on the ground. The ushers helped me to stand up and the Apostle put his hand on top of my head again while saying *"I'm doing this for your own good, my child"*. If I'm not mistaken, this process was repeated three to four times while the last two times the Apostle did not even touch me. This would turn out to be indeed a turnaround in my spiritual life. When did the service end? I have no idea, but after this day, I did not miss a service. All what would happen after this day cannot be explained by our human mind. Even me, a highly educated person, had to admit that the human mind cannot explain nor understand all of God's way.

1.6 The answer

My second attendance at a service of the church had ended with icing on top of the cake. If someone would have told me twenty four hours before or even two hours before what would happen at the service, I am sure that I would have laughed at them. That afternoon all I could do was wondering what had happened. Once the service was over, someone probably the ushers, helped me stand up and put me on a chair where I stayed for a while. I wanted to go home, but I was so dizzy, having a light feeling in my legs, in one word I felt different. What exactly was different, was hard to tell that moment, but something did feel as different. One way or another I got home, though I cannot remember how. That whole week we kept talking about the event at home. My mother in a compassionate way while my brother was teasing me by reminding me how I had said the days before the service that if I would be called to come to the front, that I would refuse to do so. Well, I was not just called to come to the front, actually the Apostle came to me, to guide me to the front. That week I started praying to God. I started slowly with small and short prayers and as the days have passed, the prayer increased in volume nevertheless remained on the short side. Till then I had not asked God the question as the Apostle and the Pastor had told me to do. I think I was afraid at that moment to pop the question for the reason that I did not know what the answer would be. On the Saturday, I was alone at home in the late afternoon and I felt the urge to start praying, so I did. I went to my room, closed the door and started with my simple prayer as I had done the days before, but suddenly it was like the burden of the last months needed to come out and I cried out to God why has my life turned out the way it was. I asked him why, if I had the perfect family and I had moved to my birthplace with the perfect plan, things were not working out the way I had planned. When would my husband join us again and so many, many other questions I had asked. After all, my crying out and questions I had posted to God, I was able to calm down and to tell God that I just had learned about him in a new way and I was not sure how He would answer me but more important I was afraid for me to make a mistake. Then I made a last request and that was for God to answer me through someone that already knew Him well and that way I would not mistake His message with false messages that might have been sent by the enemy. When I was finished, I felt a big relief and went on with the work that I was doing before I started with the praying which was cleaning up the house. My mother and brother arrived later on but I did not tell them what had happened while they were out.

The next day, Sunday, I woke up and start to prepare my children in order to be ready in time to attend service with my mother. We went to the service and experienced a lot of what I had seen in the previous services, except for my role in the last service. The service was over and I went with my mother to pick up my children at the child section. While waiting at the door, a lady whom I had not noticed before (remember this was my third visit, so how many people could I be aware of?), called my mother and when my mother turned to look at her, she asked my mother if I was her daughter by pointing out to me. My mother nodded to signal that I was her daughter. The lady turned to me and told me to come sit next to her. I had no reason not to respond to her request so I took two steps backwards in order to be able to sit next to her on a bench. Later on, I would be informed that the lady had been part of the ministry since the start and that before that she had been part of another congregation together with the Apostle and Prophet of the house. The first words the lady had said to me, made me sit straight. Her first words to me were: *"My daughter, I have a message for you from God".* Then she continued with: *"God did ask me to tell you that it He has made it possible for your husband not to join you yet. The moment will come that you will be together again, but the time has not come yet. All will be well."* The room where the child service was held was at that moment full of parents that also had come to pick up their kids but I did not notice that anymore. All I was able to do at that moment, after having heard those words, was to cry. I had seen the lady singing in the praise team without having an idea of who she was, even better she had no clue who I was as she had to ask my mother if I was her daughter, but she fulfilled what I had asked God the day before. I had asked God to answer me through someone that already knows him well. While my mind could not understand the message as it was still busy with the question how come the lady knows what I had asked God, my heart did. Can God really use someone, not the Apostle or the Pastor, but a regular person to speak to me? I went home that day wondering how God works and amazed by what had happened during my last minutes at the site of service.

CHAPTER 2

Getting to know the Holy Spirit

2.1 What is happening?

Scripture tells us in Acts 2: 1 – 4 "*When the day of Pentecost came, they were all together in one place. Suddenly a sound like the blowing of a violent wind came from heaven and filled the whole house where they were sitting. They saw what seemed to be tongues of fire that separated and came to rest on each of them. All of them were filled with the Holy Spirit and began to speak in other tongues as the Spirit enabled them*". This has always been a text to me to think about it and just that. Well, thinking about a text is another world, then living that text. I can assure you that what happened to the Apostles on the day of Pentecost is still happening nowadays. My assurance comes from the fact that I have experienced it.

After my knockout service, after all I was like five times on the ground, I did not miss a service. The strange feeling, which I felt the first time that I had attended a service, was there again at my third service, but it was accompanied by a kind of shaking of my inner body and a light shaking of my right arm. I told myself a couple of times during that service that I should not be exaggerating cause when looking around, I did not see a person with shaking body, arms or hands. I noticed that my mother noticed that my arm was acting strange. When the service was over and we were in the car, I told my mother that my arm was feeling strange during the service. She told me not to panic, that it is something that happens to some people during the service and it means that you are touched by the Holy Spirit. Well, my answer was, why did I not notice that with other people? What is that being touched by the Holy Spirit? I could not comprehend the explanation. It was so strange. In science, everything has an explanation that my mind can understand, this was for me out of all proportions. I mean, nobody had touched me, nor spoken directly to me. Why did I have the feeling that my body was shaking inside? I decided that I would definitely visit the service the week after in order to see if the same thing will happen again.

The next service that I visited not only my body was shaking inside, it was visible for others that my body and arms were shaking and I could not stop it. My mind was saying stop doing this, but my body had other coordinating mechanism because it did not do what my mind was telling it to do. It was such a strange experience. My mother kept saying to me that the Holy Spirit was working in me. All I was thinking is, oh yes? Working on what? Despite all that happened to me that my mind was not able to explain, I had a satisfying feeling in my heart. I continued to visit the services and with each service that I visited, the strange feeling (as I continued to call the feeling), was there, with each service that I experienced, the shaking of my body increased in intensity. After a couple of services I started to spin around. Why was I spinning around? I had no idea. All I knew in those moments was that a power comes up to me and it spins me around. The least pleasant part of the spinning around was that I would wake up and find myself somewhere in the room lying down. Yes, while spinning around at a certain point I smashed to the ground, however I had no idea why and had no scratches or pain. This development made it that my curiosity arose for what is happening with me. At this point I had no option than to start to accept that indeed there is something that we cannot see that influences our behavior. Could I leave it at that? Just that perception? No, I could not. I needed more information, more confirmation. There I was again with my rationalization of what is happening. I started to ask God to explain me what is happening. I had a need to understand what is happening. The answer would come from an unexpected place.

Once I started to attend the services with my mother, we also started to talk more about God and the bible at home. My mother has also given me a bible as a present on my birthday. It took a couple of months before I started to actively read the bible. At one time in a conversation she mentioned the book Good morning Holy Spirit to me. I said at that point in time, fine, I will read the book some time in the future. I was not really interested in reading the book; the bible was thick enough with a lot of information that I still had to understand. The months went by, one day I heard the name Benny Hinn from a fellow sister at the church. Then a light went on in my mind and I decided to search the internet for information on Benny Hinn. On YouTube, I found several of his videos and I started watching them. I fell into a kind of a hunger for information, so while watching the video's I did decide to start making notes. I watched one video after another. Every day, one video till I saw the video in which Benny gives a teaching on the roadmap into the presence of God[7]. There I found the answer to my question. Why was I spinning around during the services? The answer can be found in Psalm 42 verse 7. *"Deep calls to deep at the noise of your waterfalls. All your waves and your billows have swept over me."* The explanation that servant Benny provided in his teaching, was a revelation to me. Once the meaning of this landed in my mind, I said to God, *"Father, I now understand the meaning of the spinning, the way that I spin during services. If that is your will for me, I conform to it, but the falling, please remove that part"*. Soon after I noticed during services that I would be spinning around, sometimes very fast, but the falling part has come to pass. God had answered me. After this development I decided to ask my mother for the book she had mentioned months ago. From the moment I read the first page of the book Good morning Holy Spirit[8], I regretted not having read the book the moment my mother had told me about it. On the other hand, I know that the timing of God is the perfect timing. So the moment that I have read the book was the perfect moment in the timeline of God. The experiences that Benny shares in his book were for me a confirmation of my feelings during my first months in the Apostolic Prophetic Church.

2.2 The role of the family house

As explained in the earlier paragraphs, my mother was actively involved with the ministry. As my mother was blessed with the art of sewing, she was soon asked to help with the outfits for the dance ministry group. What started as a helping hand for the sewing of clothes expanded to a training center for the dance group. As the ministry did not have its own building, there was no fixed place for the dance group to practice. As the dancers came in my mother's house for cloth fitting, they noticed the patio at my mother's house that provides possibilities as a training platform for the dance group. One day, the leaders decided to ask my mother if the group can practice at her house and my mother agreed with the proposal on some conditions. So, the week there after the training started at my mother's patio. The trainings went on till one day there was a break through. Not a simple breakthrough, actually a breakthrough by the Holy Spirit. My mother was inside the house working on her stuff and suddenly she have heard some crying and screaming that she could not understand. She walked towards the window and noticed that all the dancers were lying on the ground. She went outside and walked right into the glorious presence at her house. All she could do was kneeling down and started also to cry. When I came home later that evening, I was informed of all that had happened. At that time I had been visiting the services regularly for about 6 months. I found it amazing and told my mother that her house is really blessed for that can happen there. Two weeks later, it happened again and that time I was at home. One of the leaders of the dance group came inside to ask me to come outside to join them. Even though I had been experiencing the shaking at the services, I did not expect anything to happen with me that night, after all I was at home. On that day the dancers had a white cloth that they were dancing and worshipping with and they were on the right side of the house just in front of the mango tree. That mango tree had always been full of fruits in the months of February/March and August/September. The dancers were standing more or less in a circle without holding hands and the dancer with the cloth was dancing in the middle of the circle or what was over of it. I remember that when they handed the cloth over to me and had told me to go stand in the middle, a lot of thoughts had gone through my mind. As you are standing in a circle, you tend to turn around so I started to turn around and at some point the cloth slid out of one hand so I stopped to hold it again with two hands. I heard one of the dancers say that I was breaking contact and that is why nothing was happening to me. After hearing that I took the decision that I would not let the cloth slide away again and held it firmly with both hands. Well, I made one, two, three turns and after that it was like a forced had caught the cloth because I was not the one turning and the cloth went with me, but the cloth was taking me with him. It was so hard that all I was able to do was to close my eyes and scream. At some point I opened my eyes and I was looking at the mango tree, but my view was of a person lying on the ground. I turned my head aside and noticed that indeed I had been lying on the ground. How and when did I get there? How will I be able to stand up as my body was feeling as if a bulldozer had gone through it? I had no pain. It just felt as if hours had passed by and a lot had happened while it had been only minutes. When I had turned my head on the left side, I had seen the window of my room and all I was able to say was *"Can someone carry me to my room?"* In the meanwhile, some dancers had passed through the same experience as when I managed to lift up my head, I saw some of them still lying on the ground. This was a new experience for all of us. That this would happen during a service while the Apostle was present, was considered as normal, but for it to happen in a location where the Apostle, the Pastor or the Prophet was not present and that it happened for the second time, was unknown to all. That night we all flew as the eagle described in the book of Isaiah for my mother's house is located in a street of which the name is Eagle Street *(translated)*. In the scripture of Isaiah 40:31 we are told that "*but those who hope in the Lord will renew their strength. They will soar on wings like eagles; they will run and not grow weary, they will walk and not be faint*".

Years later I would understand that even the number of the house where I grew up has a prophetic meaning. I grew up in the house located in the eagle street *(translated)* number twelve. One day that I was watching the program of ABBA House on The Church Channel of TBN, the title of the program for that day was the meaning of numbers in the kingdom of God. One of the numbers that was highlighted on that program was number twelve. Pastor Ron Philips explained in the program that the number twelve biblically represents unity, completion and the manifestation of the trinity on the earth. What had happened at my mother's house was indeed the manifestation of the Trinity what was made possible by the unity in heart of the dancers and all other present. From that moment on, I realized that my mother's house was indeed a blessed house and that it was blessed in ways we had never imagined.

2.3 The gift of tongue in operation

As time has passed by, I have matured in the knowledge and understanding of the Holy Spirit and the way God the Father, God the Son and God the Holy Spirit operate in the Apostolic Prophetic Church and the saints. I got more interested in understanding all that was happening around me and especially with me. One day my mother told me that I should long for the gift of tongue. I looked up at her and told her that longing for that is not on my mind right now, first let me understand all that is already happening. I mean, the shaking and spinning around was already enough for me. The gift of tongues can go or remain on other spiritual sisters and brothers. I did know what that the gift of tongue is, as a spiritual sister that we are very close with possesses that gift. During services when I am spinning around, I could hear her speaking in tongues. I can imagine that someone that would be visiting the service for a first time may have thought, what is happening here, because that was my first thought too on my first visit.

One day we were at my mother's house preparing for the official presentation of the CD of the praise team of the church. My mother, a spiritual sister and I were busy with the sewing of the last items, putting on the glitters and so on. The spiritual sister was sitting on the patio working with a sewing machine and I was helping my mother in her sewing room. It was a Friday night, the day of evening prayer, however we did not attend the service for the reasons mentioned above. Suddenly, my youngest brother started to call us to come quickly as he noticed that the spiritual sister was not feeling well. My mother and I stopped with what we were working on and went outside. When my mother got close by the spiritual sister, she did notice that the sister could hardly breathe. All the sister was able to say was pray for me, pray for me. My mother had asked me to call the Pastor while she started to pray for the sister. I went back inside to call the Pastor, and when he answered the phone, I explained the situation to him. All he did was listening to me and said it will be alright. Then we hung up. The prayer session was at the location nearby my mother's house so for the Pastor to arrive would not take more than five minutes. I went back outside to support my mother in prayer. After some minutes, what at that moment did seem to be hours after the call, a car was parked in front of the house. I ran to meet with the person that had arrived thinking that the person I would meet is the Pastor. When I was in front of the house I found a spiritual sister, whom is powerful in prayer, whom was sent by the Pastor. I explained the situation to her by mentioning that nothing had changed since the moment that I had spoken the Pastor. We went where my mother was praying with the sister that got sick. The sister was sitting on the chair and my mother was holding her, she looked a bit pale. We arrived at the scene and took over the prayer from my mother. We battled and battled till suddenly the sister took a deep breath and looked up at my mother and said: *"I was gone but your prayers brought me back"*. Then it was like a spiritual explosion took place, we started to thank the Lord with all of our strength and in that moment, on the patio at my mother's house, the gift of tongues came upon me. I was praying and thanking God while I suddenly started to repeat the same words, letters and so on. It was clear that it was the gift of tongues. When we had finished, thanking God for this miracle, we decided that we had to go to the prayer session. We stepped into the car the way we were dressed, with slippers on our feet and the remains of threads on our clothes. When we arrived at the prayer session, the first words of the Pastor were that we all had to believe. He had sent the sister to assist because it is not him that would have done the work but God himself. Besides, the Pastor turned to my mother and me and asked us: *"Why did you come here? For more?"* He had not even finished speaking these words and my mother and I, yes, both of us, started to spin around, the anointing was there, for sure it was there.

We stayed at the prayer session till it ended and after that we went home to finish the work that we had left.

You might be asking yourself how is it possible for that we had been working on items for the house of God and that the spiritual sister was attacked by the devil. Scripture tells us that those who serve God will be attacked. There will be trials and tribulations, but the Almighty God shall pass us through them all. (James 1: 12 and 2 Thessalonians 1: 4-7) Since that day, the gift of speaking in tongue had been operating through me. What had started with some letters and words soon flowed into sentences. Did I understand what I was saying? To be honest, no and up to this day, I still do not understand what I am saying when I am speaking in tongues, but one thing I am sure of and that is during those moments I am communicating with my heavenly father.

2.4 Let go, for God to control

As an auditor I have learned throughout my career that I had to be in control on all levels. As a student, I had to be in control of my progress, the odds of passing or not passing an exam were carefully analyzed in order to take corrective measures on time. There were courses that I did not pass at once, but on total level the results were acceptable. I finished my bachelor studies within five and a half years, followed by the master studies that took me five years to finish compared to a nominal period of four years. The master study was a part-time study that I had with my job at a Big-4 office. To be in control had to be number one while I was enrolled in the master study because it was about combining a demanding job, study and a personal life. All of this had not been different from my fellow students or persons that had done the same study elsewhere in the world. Working at a Big-Four company has always been demanding, but in the years that the economy was booming, a lot of professionals of the big four companies received offers that were too good to refuse so that they left to the fulfill functions in different businesses. Throughout the years, a shift in the mindset of the public in general was noticeable making work-life balance more and more important. Consequently the inflow of students into the auditing and consulting firms started to decrease slowly but noticeably.

So as I had been explaining, I was used to be in control of everything. When I accepted Jesus in my life as my Savior and I had noticed the way that the Holy Spirit operates through man, I had to make a decision. I had to decide if I would remain in control of myself, my being and everything else or if I would give the control to the Holy Spirit, to Jesus. Because of all that had happened or even what had not happened the way I had planned for, I had contemplated that I had nothing more to lose by handing it all over to the Holy Spirit. The day that the aforementioned reflection and conclusion had gone across my mind, is the day that I took the decision to be baptized. The day that I had taken that decision was at a service where for the countless times I could not stand or sit still. I took a seat that day on a chair in the middle of the room. I would say far enough from the front and kind of hidden behind the other people present. I was trembling all over my body and the service had just started! My body was shaking that much that I had to grip the border of the chair in order to not fall off from the chair. My silent prayer was, let the Pastor not take notice of this, but as everyone went to sit down quietly, the overwhelming sound that came out from the back was that of my legs smacking against each other. The Pastor stopped with his preaching in order to ask my neighbor is everything is ok back there. Was everything ok? I had no idea if I had to say it is ok or not after all I could not sit still due to the manifestation of the Holy Spirit. The Pastor decided to call me to the front. Walking to the front was an experience on its own as the ushers had to support me. Once in the front, the Pastor had asked me what I want. All I was able to say at that moment was that I wanted to be baptized. A year later, a week before my birthday, I was baptized. Why did it take so long? I guess that my mind needed some time to adjust to the need of my spirit.

I was part of a group of six to ten people that had indicated that they wanted to be baptized during those days. We had been told to reunite for Morning Prayer at 5 a.m. and that after the prayer session we would head for the baptismal site. The baptize site is a small beach located on the northeast side of the island and is famous for the nature that surrounds it. There you can see the sun coming up from the horizon; you can hear the birds sing and the waves smashing into the rocks. On this site, there is a small bay where the water is calm and perfect for swimming or baptizing. As we were told, we reunited that Saturday morning and we had a powerful Morning Prayer session. Then we went, accompanied by some spiritual brother and sisters that did come to support, to the small beach nearby where the Pastor and a spiritual brother headed into the water and they did stand still when they were up to their waist into the salty water. The Pastor then started to call us one by one to walk towards them in the water. I noticed that the brothers and sisters that went before me, were held by the Pastor and the brother at their shoulder and were helped when they went backwards under the water and up again on their feet. On my turn I walked into the water and on the indication of the Pastor I stood still in between the Pastor and the brother with my face towards the shore. For some reason I closed my eyes. While standing there in the water, a strange feeling started to capture me and then I heard the Pastor telling me not to withstand it. Just after he had spoken those words, I felt my left hand making some moves and I went backwards into the water. When I was under the water I felt one strong hand on my back, pushing me up and I was again on both of my feet. I opened my eyes, took a look at the Pastor and went on to walk towards the shore. Once on shore, I joined the brothers and sisters in prayer as a support for the ones that still had to be baptized. Once finished, the Pastor and the spiritual brother whom was helping him, came to shore and we had one closing prayer in which we all thanked God for the moment and all the great things that would follow. Then we started to exchange experiences of the moments when we were in the water. I turned to one of the sisters that were present to support the baptism and I did remark that I really had felt when the Pastor and the brother had pushed me up from under the water. The sister did turn to look at me and said to me *"None of them touched you. You went down alone and you came up alone"*. My reaction was: *"Are you sure? Because I really, really had felt a hand pushing me up when I was under the water."* She replied to me that she had been looking at the moment of my baptism and she had not seen the hand of the Pastor nor the brother move. None of them had helped me to go backwards into the water nor had they helped me to come up out of the water. I was so amazed by the information that she had provided to me, that the next day I had asked her the question again. I guess I wanted to make sure that she was sure of her statement. As could be expected, she has given the same declaration and finalized with the statement that what I had felt must have been the Holy Spirit himself. Well, that was something to think about.

2.5 Holy mathematics

There is one course that all highly educated once had in their student time and that is mathematics. As preferences are different for each person, some had loved it and other would have preferred to throw it away. OECD has been conducting the Programme for International Student Assessment (PISA) since 1997. One of the areas on which the PISA focusses is mathematics. For the PISA 2012[9] the following definition has been used by OECD for mathematical literacy: "*Mathematical literacy is an individual's capacity to formulate, employ, and interpret mathematics in a variety of contexts. It includes reasoning mathematically and using mathematical concepts, procedures, facts and tools to describe, explain and predict phenomena. It assists individuals to recognise the role that mathematics plays in the world and to make the well-founded judgments and decisions needed by constructive, engaged and reflective citizens*". I agree with the point of view that knowledge of mathematical concepts is essential nowadays. The fact that we have a huge amount of information to process on a daily basis is eminent. I would add to it that the highly educated individuals that function in top positions in the corporate and social domain, have proportionately a higher percentage of information to process on a daily basis when considering the expectations that we, as humans, have set in terms of expected response time on e-mails, calls and not to forget the countless meetings on a weekly basis. By applying mathematical concepts, we are able to manage the information flow and requests that we receive. The definition for mathematical literacy might be interpreted as that mathematics can only be applied in the natural world. Actually, I have learned in the last four that there is another level of mathematics, there is the holy mathematics. At secondary school all students learn that the basis for mathematics is X+Y=Z. It does not matter in which field you are, this is the basic mathematic. It gets more complicated when a third variable is added to the equation to become X+Y+V=Z. When adding a fourth or fifth variable it gets even more complicated. Complexity and mathematics are therefore seen as interrelated concepts. I would describe holy mathematics as an equation that consist of only three variables and therefore not that much complicated. The equation for the holy mathematics is P+P+P=P and it stands for Prayer + Praise + Pure heart equals the Presence, the Holy Presence. In the math class at college or university, actually even at the primary school, you learn that math is a subject that requires trial and error efforts. For the holy math I would not say it is a matter of trial and error, but rather a matter of adjusting the tone. Are you praying with a sincere heart? Does the praise come from within your heart and soul? Are you ready to put your heart on the table for Jesus? If the answer is yes to all these questions, then you will flow into worship what is the key to unlock the door to heaven for the Holy Presence to manifest in and through you. Adjusting the tone is not easy, but not impossible. It requires dedication and patience. Once you understand how the equation works, you should practice and practice in order to enhance your skills in the holy mathematics. I am telling you this as this has been the way that I was able to understand the manifestation of the Holy Spirit.

CHAPTER 3

The Holy Spirit in the lead

3.1 The anointing for dancing

As I was born in the Caribbean, on the island of Curaçao, music and dancing have always been two of my favorites. Whether it is a salsa, merengue or a waltz, all are welcome. I have always enjoyed being on my personal dance floor, where I am able to do the moves that I like and the critics can only come from the mirror. Though I liked music very much I was never a party fever type. A public party once in a while was good enough for me. There was a radio station with a sweet popular program every Saturday morning and I used to listen to that program. While helping my mother sweep the floor, the radio would be at an almost full level for me to enjoy the music. There was a period on the island that gospel songs were very popular and I enjoyed singing them in the car or at home.

There is a salsa song which I enjoyed in the early 1990's whom I did not expect of myself that I would still know the refrain in two thousand and eleven. One day while sitting at the dinner table and talking with my mother about situations which had happened at work, I started to sing the song as it came to me suddenly. The refrain of the song, which is a Spanish song, says

"Hay quien pasa su vida en el fondo de una botella.
Hay quien cree que inflando sus venas podria volar.
Esa no es la manera mas sabia de hallar la respuestá.
No es lo mismo llamar al demoño que ver lo llegar."[10]

Translated to English it says: Some spend their lives drinking from a bottle. Some think that by putting air into their veins that they could fly. That is not the way to find the answers. It is not the same to call onto the devil as seeing him arrive

She asked me why I was singing that song. I answered that it just came up in my mind so I started to sing it. I continued telling her that when reflecting on all of the situations, including my discovery of the new me in Christ, the songwriter had it right by saying that none of the answers can be found in the earthly things. The spiritual world is as real as the table that we were sitting at on that moment and that talking about the spiritual world and having experienced the spiritual are indeed two different things. One thing I was sure of at that moment and that was that I would prefer all the challenges that God would put me through to in order to mold me and form me than to be with the enemy. For I know, that God's blessings shall come after the challenges and that He will not leave from my side during the challenges and trials.

When I joined the church in late two thousand and ten, the sister that had provided me with the answer, as described in paragraph 1.6, commented to my mother and a spiritual sister that we are very close to, that I had been called to dance for the Lord. This information was not revealed to me until after my baptism. When I had heard this information, there could be no doubt anymore that indeed that is one of the reasons I was called for. From the moment I had joined the church my body had been shaking as if I had been in a washing machine when the spin cycle is on. This shaking soon developed into hands that would make several movements to continue to my whole body spinning around in the room. With every service this power intensified, so that I could not ignore it. When I tried to ignore it, it felt as if an explosion was taking place inside of me. I had to release this power and the only way to do so was by dancing, by spinning around. Oh, what a relief was felt after spinning around. The feeling inside was more than what my body could handle. It was as if it was asking to be spread among the people.

After this I had three experiences, each on another day yet all were one of a kind in the way the Holy Spirit and the Angels of God manifest on this earth. When I joined the congregation, we had no fixed location. We were moving from one place to another, yet we did not bother as each and every service was filled with joy, power and manifestation of the Holy Spirit. When it is known beforehand that we have to change location on a Sunday, this would be communicated during or at the end of the service the previous week. It happened a few times that the leaders found the surprise in the middle of the week or sometimes even on Friday, that the location is not available. The Apostle encouraged the congregation to listen each Sunday to a specific radio program, for in case there is a change in the location of the service. Two of the services which we had in the location that is actually a former plantation, as we would say in the local language "hofi", was enlightening for me. The service had been going on and the presence of the Holy Spirit was evident as the wind that was blowing through the leaves of the mango and medlar trees in the plantation. At a certain point the Apostle looked at the congregation and said in his own words that the acceptation and the reaction of the congregation must be better. He turned to me, as that day I had been sitting in front at the left side, and asked me when I would start while showing me with his hands to stand up. In all honesty, I did not understand him at that moment. I was confused, as in the earlier part of the service I had been shaking; I mean, that was for me a usual thing during a service. After making these statements, the Apostle left the site to go worship at his special site. The service continued and it was as if the words of the Apostle made a change in the spiritual realm. Once the worship songs started to flow again, it was as if a spiritual sauce had been spread over the congregation. Suddenly, the members of the dance ministry group started to dance and I found myself moving on the platform and I could not stop my body. It was prophetic dance in a way which I had only seen one person doing at the service, our mother in prophetic dance. In one sentence, the service ended with a tremendous spiritual climax.

There was another occasion at the same location where the service was led by the Pastor. That day again, we had powerful prayers, worship and manifestations of the Holy Spirit. Once more I was sitting in the front, but this time more in the middle. The end of the service was approaching and the Pastor was making some final remarks while we were standing and applauding. The Pastor suddenly told the congregation that despite the fact that we are finalizing the service, if needed he could call on the angels of God to come and perform the work of God. I cannot tell you exactly what happened the moment those words were spoken, yet I can tell you that I felt a force moving me forward towards the platform, turning me around in a circle and bringing me back to the location where I was standing before it all started. All that time I had my eyes closed and did not fall. Once, standing again in front of my seat, breathing heavily as you can imagine, it all happened in a short couple of minutes. The Pastor continued with his closing remarks and a couple of minutes after I was standing again at my location when the service ended. Me? I was glad that I could take a seat to recover of the last action of the Holy Spirit and the angels of God through me, for that particular service. Once again, God had shown me that He shall use the person that He decides and at the moment that He decides. Can all of this be explained by the human nature and logic? All the logic of physics that I had learned and remembered, does not explain it. Can any of the theories which you learned in college or university explain it? I doubt it. If you think that I'm wrong, tell me if the following experience can be captured within the theories that are taught in schools.

One day during a service, the Apostle was preaching about revival. That day he called several people to the front and prayed with them. In one of the rounds that he was calling people by pointing at them, he called me too. Together with ten people, I was standing in the front. He prayed for all of us individually and then continued with either a blow in the face of a person, a hand touch to the person's head and so on. He left me as the last one of the group. I was standing there in anticipation of what he would be saying and/or doing to me. Then he came to stand in front of me, took both of my hands in his hand, while he was looking at the people standing on his left hand. Suddenly he told them to go back in order to make some space. As the people did not go as far as he had wanted, he showed them again that they had to make some space. I could not understand what was happening or what would happen. Then the Apostle made a swinging movement with his hands while holding my hands and went on to let my hands go. The next thing I know is that I was spinning around very fast, but this time with my eyes open. Normally when you spin around with your eyes open, you start to feel dizzy immediately. Well, that moment in the service all I was feeling was an urge to dance. My hands were moving and making shapes I could not understand with my mind, my feet were turning me around in ways that I could have never imagined. Like a week of two later I had the courage to ask a spiritual sister, a member of the praise team whom has been serving the Lord for years, the meaning of what had happened at the service. I had a good understanding with her as she had been the one through whom God had spoken to me the first time. The sister informed me that the anointing of dancing was imparted on me that day. Again, something to think about.

3.2 Calling for the seraphim's

In my search for more and more information on the kingdom of God and the way it operates, I found information on the existence of the different types of angels. Again, it was a teaching of Benny Hinn, a servant of God, which informed me and opened my eyes on this matter. I have to admit that I was very intrigued by the existence and function of the seraphim's, the angels of adoration. I made my notes and went back to them for a couple of days. I had even read the scriptures that were mentioned during the teaching session. I had taught that the information on the seraphim's and their continuous adoration towards God might be useful in the next main service that I would attend.

The days had passed by and it became Sunday. We prepared for the service and arrived at the service. My children have gone to the children session and I took place at the right hand of the room around the middle. Praise and worship started to flow and filled the room. I remembered the teaching on the seraphim's and wanted to test to see if what was said is true. After all, a highly educated is always in search for proof of what has been said or told is true, aren't we? While the praise songs were filling the room, I closed my eyes and said to myself: "God, could you please release your seraphim's for them to take our praise and worship up to your throne?" The moment I finished saying this, I felt like a power took over my body. I started to dance while the praise and worship was flowing. This time the feeling was somehow different from the times before. All I was able to think about, was that it was indeed a blessing to be able to dance together with the seraphim's in praise and worship for our mighty God. From that day on, I kept asking God to release his seraphim's as we were praising and worshipping him and the response I receive is always one of power.

Within one and a half year my understanding and view of the kingdom of God had completely changed in a way that I could have never imagined before.

3.3 Praying sessions at home

After my first start with prayer under the new knowledge, and after the result of my initial prayer and supplication, I gained more confidence in my prayer and I continued to pray every day. In order to make sure that I would pray and read from the bible, I made it part of the bedtime routine for my children. After changing clothes and brushing the teeth we would say together a prayer and I would read a text from the bible. My children started full of enthusiasm and on day two they already had some moves to take me out of my concentration. A change of tactics was needed. I changed the set up to where I would say the prayer, they would repeat it and when finished, I would put them in bed in order to continue with the reading of a small portion out of the bible. This setup was wonderful except for the fact that for the children to repeat an impromptu prayer is more difficult than expected. Then I finally decided to go for a standard prayer and we ended up repeating every day the prayer that Jesus had told his disciples in Matthew 6:9-13. "*This, then, is how you should pray: "'Our Father in heaven, hallowed be your name, your kingdom come, your will be done, on earth as it is in heaven. Give us today our daily bread. And forgive us our debts, as we also have forgiven our debtors. And lead us not into temptation, but deliver us from the evil one."*

It worked perfectly as when we finished with the prayer, I would go over to read a text from the bible. The best part of all is that while I was reading, they would fall asleep. Did each day go as simple? Oh, no. One day they would decide to play while repeating the prayer and another day they would decide not to repeat at all. On those days, I would take a deep breath and continue with the bedtime routine. After a while I noticed that even though the children would be playing when I was saying the prayer, their mind caught up what I was saying. How did I notice? Well, they would tell me that what I prayed was the same as a couple of days before. I was surprised and then realized that as long as I continued to feed them spiritually, they would receive it. After all, can you expect for a kid of two years old and another one of four years old to sit quietly? I continued with this routine, although there were some days that we skipped either because I was extremely tired or they had fallen asleep in the car. When I'm extremely tired, my routine would change to where I would be lying in bed and I would just do a short prayer. It could be as short as, thank you Adonai for this day as long as fifteen minutes or half an hour. Despite all circumstances, I would say a prayer each and every day. After a while I started to notice a change. I started to notice that while reading the text of the bible, the inside of my body started to feel as shaking as when I am in a service. I told myself not to exaggerate. One day, while the children were still awake, I had opened the bible at the text of the Pentecost in Acts 2:1-4 that says: "*When the day of Pentecost came, they were all together in one place. Suddenly a sound like the blowing of a violent wind came from heaven and filled the whole house where they were sitting. They saw what seemed to be tongues of fire that separated and came to rest on each of them. All of them were filled with the Holy Spirit and began to speak in other tongues as the Spirit enabled them.*" As I read the text and I came to the part where the tongues of fire had descended on the Apostles, I just felt the shaking inside my body and my speaking turned into speaking in tongues. There, in the bedroom of my children with the curtains and doors closed, where no one except my children could see me, I was speaking in tongue. When I was finished, my daughter asked me: "*Mama, what was that?*" I tried the best way that I could at that moment to explain it to a five year old. The week thereafter and the week that followed, I had the same experience and at both times, the children were still awake. If you ask my children now, what happens when we pray at home, they start to laugh and then they say: *"mama starts always to say....."* and they start imitating me. I can be happy because my children have seen the signs and wonders of Adonai. They will grow up knowing that the Almighty lives and He is the only one that they should bow to and fear. He is holy and worthy to be praised. Up to this day on occasions that the Holy Spirit decides that it is needed, the Holy Presence is (frequently) present in my home during the evening praying sessions.

3.4 Obedience is a key

For this part, I have to take you back to the beginning of the story and that is to the role of my mother. As I had explained in chapter one, my mother had been in obedience to God, even when she had not known this. How do I know that she had obeyed? Well, in a quite unusual way for me, yet planned by God this information was revealed to us. Ten and a half years after the family tragedy, I was on my way to a new year's afternoon celebration of a company. I was invited to a company's year-end informal celebration and thou I had a new view on the whole new year celebration in December, what is the result of the education received at the congregation, I planned to attend the celebration. Before attending the celebration, I had a conversation with God at home as part of a prayer. I had said to God that I know that this is not part of the celebrations that He had instituted, but if He wanted me to do the work that I assumed that He wanted me to do, and then I must be in contact with professionals also on informal occasions. I continued then by saying to God, that where I am going there will be music and it would look very odd if someone ask me to dance for me to say no every time, so what I am asking Him is if someone does ask me to dance please to let it be only when a song is playing that would not harm the holy kingdom nor his children in the spiritual realm. After this prayer, I went to the celebration with the expectation that I would not dance. On the other hand, once you experience dancing with the Holy Spirit, believe me, there is no dancing that is more fulfilling than that. Soon I arrived as the distance was very short and I noticed that on the patio at the side of the office building a podium was set up for a live band performance, a disk jockey was playing music and it was not too crowded. I socialized with those that were present and got an invitation to dance and to my surprise, the song that was playing at that moment, I could not have been happier with. The song was about a new year that is bringing light into the life of those that live in the darkness. A song written and played in the natural that reflects the spiritual realm as it is, God bringing light into our lives. After a while at the celebration, I decided to return home. The moment I entered the car, I said thank you father for you had answered my prayer and I had been able to fulfill my social obligation. I was behind the wheel, waiting at a traffic light when an idea passed through my mind. The plan that came up suddenly was to walk towards my mother when I arrive at her place and to tell her that it is because she had obeyed, the plan to save Curaçao would be executed. What a strange thought, was the next thing that came into my mind, but the last one was erased by the earlier thought that came up again. Then I said, still on the road heading for home, "God, if this is your will, I will do so even though I do not understand it". Once at home, I parked the car and headed to the door of the apartment on my mother's premises where a spiritual sister lives. When I knocked, she opened very quickly and I asked her if she can accompany me to my mother because I had a message to tell her and I need some support. Support for what? I had no clue. She replied to me that just before I had entered the premises with the car she had already felt the presence of the Holy Spirit arrive. All I could say to her then is, well then I definitely have to tell my mother what I have on my heart, as the word had come down from my mind to my heart. So, the two of us walked from her front door, turned the corner to the front door of my mother's house. We noticed that the door was closed so we went to the patio of my mother's house and when we turned the corner I started to call my mother. She came out to meet us in the middle of the patio, yes the same patio where the other manifestations of the Holy Spirit happened. When I was standing in front of my mother and I opened my mouth, it was as if heaven had come down on me. I felt such a presence of the Holy

Spirit that I could barely continue talking. My mother had to hold me for me not to fall on the ground. I tried again to speak and was able to tell her what the Holy Spirit had told me in the car, because by then I had no doubt that it was the Holy Spirit and definitely not my own desire. My mother started to cry and asked me where I had been. *"Had you been at the house of the Apostle and the Prophet? Have you spoken to the Prophet on the phone? Have you seen one of them or the Pastor on your way home?"* All questions that I had to answer with one word, NO. The Holy presence was so evident to all the three of us that afternoon on the patio that you could almost touch it. My mother and I cried together there on the patio as we could not understand the magnitude of and the exact reason for the words, but one thing we could not deny and that was the Holy presence. The spiritual sister got her portion too, as she told me half an hour later that the moment I parked the car on the premises all her body started to shake. How great is our God and how spectacular are the ways that He works. In all of this we are only the vessels that He uses for His name to be glorified.

3.5 A prophecy for Curaçao

In the Bible, we can read all the prophecies that had been spoken by the Prophets in the ancient times. It may sound awkward in the ears of a highly educated, yet as up today prophecies are given to the Prophets in order for them to share these with the congregations and nations. This is not something only of the past. No. God has anointed and appointed His servant throughout the world to speak of His word and to communicate prophecies. I am not the expert to tell you how and when you can expect a prophecy, still based on my experience up until now I would say that the Prophet does not know the prophecy until the moment it is revealed to him or her.

A prophecy has been revealed for my place of birth, the island Curaçao. At the time that this prophecy had been released, I was not yet a member of the Apostolic Prophetic Church. Since my membership at the church I have heard the prophecy, as it was released, a couple of times. My mother was present at the service in which the prophecy had been released and she confirmed to me the words that I had heard concerning the prophecy.

In two thousand and nine, the word of God had come upon one of his servants to speak out to the Apostolic and Prophetic Congregation on Curaçao that the time will come that nations will be coming to the island to see what is happening there on a spiritual level. How and when shall be revealed to the servants of God on the island that are walking in the dimension in which Adonai is operating. When I look back at my experiences as described in the previous chapters and paragraphs, all I can say is that I have truly experienced that the Word of God shall not return back to Him before completing with the purpose for which it has been released (Isaiah 55:11). This will surely count for the prophecy that has been spoken for Curaçao. This is only a recording of the prophecy for when the moment that it is fulfilled, we all again can bow down our knees and declare the greatness of God that we cannot capture with our minds.

CHAPTER 4

Anointing in The Netherlands

4.1 Introduction

In the previous chapter you have read how the Holy Spirit had been working in and through my life when I was on the island of Curaçao. As I had indicated in chapter one, I moved to the island without my husband with the expectation that he would soon follow for our family to be complete again. The plan of God with my life was not what I had expected. After ten months on the island, I had joined the Apostolic Prophetic Church where I had been experiencing the amazing manifestation of the presence of the Holy Spirit. Three years later, my husband was still living in The Netherlands, while the children and I were still on the island. During that period he had flown regularly between the island and the Netherlands in order to be with us. Nevertheless, it was not easy for him to miss the stages in the development and growth of our children, he had not been complaining. He was happy for me that I was experiencing God in a new way, but for him, no change was needed. For me, that was a familiar point of view, a point where I had been standing before.

As God had let me to the text in 1 Corinthians 7:5 as a confirmation that I was on the right path, I still had the hope that soon, very soon my husband would find the job on the island. That hope started to vanish the day the Apostle asked me for my husband and in his own particular style he had asked me when I would be returning to The Netherlands. It was a Sunday, the service had finished and my mother and I were fellowshipping shortly with some sisters and brothers when the Apostle had walked me by, stopped and asked me the question. *"Returning to The Netherlands?"* I replied. He looked up at me, smiled and walked away. There I was with the question marks in my mind. Why God? Why do I have to return? Why can't you let him come this way? Why? Why?

On our way home, my mother and I did not talk about the remark of the Apostle, probably because we both had felt in which direction the message was going. I tried to ignore the message and kept trying to get a job for my husband on the island. About two to three months later, the Apostle asked me again when I would be returning to The Netherlands in a more drastic manner. Then I had to comfort myself that this is indeed the will of God. After accepting this, I started to make all arrangements for our return to The Netherlands. My husband took care of the arrangements in The Netherlands like social security, school for the children and so on. Time had passed by and the week had come for us to depart. Just, one last service on the island.

That last service for me on the island was full of the Holy Presence. When the service was reaching its end the Apostle had called all persons that had a birthday in the last week. I went also the front for a prayer as I would depart on the Tuesday. While I was standing in the front awaiting my turn, I noticed that the Prophet, my spiritual mother, approached a servant that was visiting from The Netherlands to come and pray for me. This Pastor started to pray for me and I closed my eyes as I started to feel a bubbling inside of me. Then I heard the Pastor asking me to open my eyes and look up to him. Well, the moment I did what I was asked to do, I felt my body starting to dance. I was dancing, turning around, moving away from the Pastor and making use of the space that was available. When I was able to stand still, I went back to the initial position where I was standing. Then the Apostle of the house came to me and asked me why I came for a prayer whereupon I replied that I would be returning to The Netherlands that week. He then nodded with his head, said that it was ok and for me to remain standing there. After some minutes he came back, he laid his hand on my head and prayed for me. He told me *"All will be well, my child. All will be well"*.

4.2 Back at the start?

A week before my departure to The Netherlands I had called the Apostle to inform where I was allowed to attend service in The Netherlands. It was not a matter that he would restrict me, but I had learned that consulting with your spiritual father and mother before taking steps is for your own protection. So, I called the Apostle and I posted the question if it is ok for me to attend a church that was about half an hour from my home in The Netherlands. His reply to me was *"No, do not go there. I will check for you where you can go and I will let you know"*. Up to today, I did not receive the aforementioned information from the Apostle. Initially I was upset about it. Later on I would understand that he had taken a step backwards for me to receive directions directly from the Most High.

So there I was again in The Netherlands after a period of three and a half years. Years in which I had learned that God the Father, God the Son and God the Holy Spirit are not only written in the bible. What do you do after having passed through all that I had already shared with you? My family is finally as it is supposed to be, all happy together, however the Apostolic Prophetic Community I had been part of is not nearby. I pondered, is this it? All the experiences with the Holy Spirit to let it all end up in nothing, or as we say on the island, "aros y coco" meaning rice and coconut. I refused to accept that. The first two weeks I had prayed every day asking Adonai for direction. I knew that the Apostolic Congregation of Curaçao had dependencies at that time in four cities in The Netherlands yet the closest one was about forty five minutes away. Although there were a lot of alternatives in my town, I did not feel it in my spirit to attend one of them. Does it mean that those congregations are not good enough? Not at all. I have learned from my spiritual father and mother that Adonai works through several channels. As our body constitutes of feet, hands, head and all other small details, so is the body of Christ represented through the churches. Each congregation has a mandate to complete with and so do we as servants. My calling is bound to the Apostolic Prophetic Congregation where I started till Adonai decides otherwise. This particular fact was not in my mind a year and a half ago. What I did instead was praying to Adonai for a convenient solution and while waiting for the convenient solution, I decided to attend the service of the sister congregation in Amsterdam which was the closest for me.

I decided on Saturday that the next day I would attend the service in Amsterdam. All the people I had called to ask them for the address and the time of the service did not pick up. I went on to look on the internet and Facebook for information. By chance I noticed an announcement of the service location, so far no notification of the weekday or time. I said to Adonai, you have told me on Curaçao that all will be well, so do not let me down. I will go for it that the service is on Sunday at 10 am. The next morning I woke up early, made all preparations for the children and myself to attend a service. My husband did not find it necessary for him to attend and I did not question that. I took the car, programmed the navigation system and up to Amsterdam. After forty five minutes and a couple of extra turns we arrived at the parking location indicated by the navigation system. I parked the car and took a look around, where am I supposed to go? To the left, right, north or south? I had no clue. The idea came up in me to call my mother as she had attended the services in Amsterdam two years before, she might remember in which building the services are held. When I called her, I got the surprise of my life. Her first remark was *"Are you in Amsterdam? But the services there are held on Saturday."* There I was, sitting in the car all the way in Amsterdam to hear that the service took place the day before. I took a deep breath while I contemplated that I had prayed to Adonai to not let me down. I just refused to believe that He had let me come all the way to Amsterdam while the service had taken place the day before." So I replied to my mother, *"Are you sure that the service is on Saturday?"* She replied by saying that so was the case two years ago, yet the best thing I could do is try to reach my aunt to ask her as she might know. While talking to my mother, I noticed that a car was approaching and it parked next to me. When I saw who was in the car, I could only praise the Lord. In the car that had just parked next to us, had arrived the Prophet of the Amsterdam Congregation with her daughter of four years old and two other people whom I did not know. I told my mother that all is well, as I got people to lead me to the service and hung up the phone. We stepped quickly out of the car to join the group that was heading to the service location. While we were walking to the location, the Prophet told me that her daughter started to scream in the car *"mama, mama there are the kids from Curaçao"*. The Prophet and her children had been indeed in Curaçao and they had returned to The Netherlands one week before we did. The children had not seen each other for over three weeks, but the connection was there immediately as they had seen each other again.

Finally, after two weeks in The Netherlands, I had the opportunity to attend a service. When we arrived at the service site, the praise was already started under the guidance of the evangelist. I was welcomed by the ushers and took a seat in the fourth row right on the aisle. I had expected that this would be a service in which I would have a chance to start over again after all I had moved from Curaçao to The Netherlands and I had not been to a service for over two weeks. After thirty minutes of presence at the location, with the praise and worship flowing into the room, I started to feel as old. My body was overwhelmed by the Holy Presence and a desperate need to start to dance captured me. I tried to suppress the feeling, but at the end the presence was so overwhelming that I started to dance. What a relief that was. The ushers whom did not know me yet, came immediately towards me with the intention to protect me. The evangelist took a look and me and said to the usher *"Leave her. Let her dance!"* Once those words were spoken, it was as if the heaven opened further upon me. The worship was flowing and so was the Holy Spirit through me. I may have considered when I had arrived in The Netherlands that I was back at the start nevertheless at that single moment I had realized that I was not back at the start, this is merely the continuation. The continuation of what, was still to be revealed.

4.3 Wings of fire

My mother, who had stopped working in order to stay home with her children, is a woman that has been blessed with many talents. One of these talents is the making and sewing of outfits. From baby clothes to suits, from simple dresses to bridal gowns. I have seen her making all of them. As I had helped her once in a while with some simple tasks, like picking up the needles from the ground and sweeping the remainders of threads and fabrics as well as sewing on a button, I had learned bit by bit the tips and tricks of the job. As I had indicated in chapter one, my mother had been busy with the sewing of dancing dresses for the dance ministry group of the congregation. Besides the dresses, she had been making also standard flags and dancing flags, the so called half circle angel wings. Even though my mother was the one making the flags, I had never asked her to make one for me while I was in Curaçao so when I moved back to The Netherlands, I did not have a set of half circle angel wings.

After my first service in Amsterdam, I continued to visit the services there while waiting for the moment that Adonai would tell me to move to a congregation that is closer to home. Each and every service that I had visited was powerful. One night when I had just laid my head on the pillow and closed my eyes, I saw myself dancing with gold colored half circle angel wings. I opened my eyes immediately, took a look around and concluded that I had just imagined it. I went on to sleep. Two days later, I had the same experience, only this time I had a close up view of the fabric of which the wings were made. The fabric was gold colored semitransparent with a thick gold colored thread passing across it. It was the fabric of a curtain I had seen two months before in the store, which I had the intension to buy, but on second thought I did not. That night I decided that I had to go back to the store to buy the fabric. When I went to the store there was only one piece left of the curtain. I held it in my hand and was wondering why Adonai wants me to use this fabric. As I did not have the answer yet, I bought the item and went home to figure out how I would be making the flags.

The week thereafter, when I had arrived at the service, I had the half circle angel wings with me. I walked to a sister that also is regularly touched by the Holy Spirit for dancing, and I told her that I have something for her to test. Once the service was started and the sister started to dance under the guidance of the Holy Spirit, my eyes went to her hands. Her hands were in the position for holding angel wings. I turned to take the wings I had made and handed them over to her. What a joy I had that moment when seeing her dancing with the wings. From that moment on, I would take the wings to every service I attend. Services would follow where I was dancing with the wings, I would feel the impulse to hand over the wings to a sister. What would happen when I hand over the wings is just indescribable. It is as if the anointing passes over from the wings to the person. On other occasions I had felt the urge to stop dancing with the wings, walk towards a sister and just go lightly with the wings over the head of the person. The first time I had felt this need, I had found it very strange and I even wanted not to do it. Then again, I felt the need increase inside of me and I said in myself *"Father, I do not want to do anything on my own or out of my own idea. If this is not yours, let me know"*. As nothing had happened except for that the urge further increased inside of me, I decided to walk towards the person and go lightly with the wings from right to left and from left to right over her head. The second time that I was instructed by the Holy Spirit to do the aforementioned routine, I got curious. After the service, I walked to the concerning sister to ask her if something had happened the moment I had passed the wings lightly over her head. The reaction that I received makes me truly understand that my action was not directed by my mind though purely by the Holy Spirit.

4.4 What a revelation

In the month of May two thousand and fourteen, a women's conference was held in the city of Breda, The Netherlands. At that time I had been living again in the Netherlands for like six months. All women of the several locations of our congregation in The Netherlands, were invited to attend. In order to keep the costs of attendance low, we made plans for carpooling. As I had a lease car at my disposal, I offered to pick up sisters that would be able to take the train to a location on my route to Breda. At the end I made arrangements with one sister to pick her up and so did I. In the car we started talking about our expectation for the day and we also talked about the women's conferences that had been held in the past. During the conversation, as we had to drive about one hour and fifteen minutes, we started to talk about how we joined this congregation. The sister told me her story first and then I went on with mine. While talking I started to tell her about a specific period in my time at the congregation, being the time in between the period that I started to attend the church services and the period that I had fully accepted that God is calling me to make a difference in this world. That was for me the period of doubt and questions. Doubt because it is easy to ask myself if I am sure that God had called you to serve him in such away, after all I had not aspired to become a Prophet or so. I had questions, because I had seen a lot of persons who had been attending the services long before me, but they are not touched in the way that I was touched by the Holy Spirit during services.

I continued to tell the sister that there had been a couple of services were the Apostle emphasized the importance of arriving early at the service site and to start with personal prayer before the actual start of the service. He explained that the angels prepare the service site before we arrive and that those who arrive early do get the fruit of their efforts. After hearing this calling for early attendance like three to four times and being touched the way I had been describing that I was touched by the Holy Spirit, I thought that I had found the perfect plan. Rather arriving early at the service site, I would be late on purpose, so the Holy Spirit would use those that are present before me. The sister laughed at this remark and asked me if I completed the plan. I told her that indeed that I had done it, but the result was far from what I had expected. The sister asked me: *"What do you mean?"* I went on to tell her that the times that I had arrived late on purpose at a service were only two. Why so little? Simply because on those two occasions, the minute I had put my feet into the room, I was arrested by the Holy Spirit that at the end of the service I would be sitting on the side gasping for air and asking someone what was actually preached that day as I had been either shaking, spinning around or talking in tongue for the most time I had been present. I was so drunk of the Holy Spirit that I could not understand it. The sister listened to me with attention, then she started to laugh and she said: *"didn't the Apostle tell you at the beginning that you think you are smart? Now you see why. You thought that arriving late at service would be a great idea, but God had another plan."* Her question and her remark had shocked me. There in the car, riding on the highway in The Netherlands, I received the answer to the question that had been bothering me since day one that I had set my feet at a service of this ministry in Curaçao. After three and a half years I understood the remark of the Apostle. What a revelation this has been to me.

4.5 The way forward

The Apostolic Prophetic Congregation where I started and continue to form part of, has advanced as her leaders have advanced in the spiritual realm by means of prayer, praise, worship, dedication to the word of Adonai and communion with the Holy Spirit. This congregation is now a Messianic Community, to be precise the *Rains of Blessings for All Nations Messianic Community*, proclaiming the word of revival among the nations based on the promises in the word of Adonai and the revelations that Adonai is giving to the leaders. A Messianic Community or congregation[11] explains the Gospel of Jesus from the Jewish context. The difference between a messianic community and a Christian church lies in the fact that the messianic community works from the calendar, customs and perspective of the Jewish community what adds a dimension that is not found in other Christian traditions[12].

A year ago I was asking Adonai why I had to return to The Netherlands. Now I know. I, as a highly educated, have the task to help with the setup and further professionalization of this Messianic Community. This fact was revealed to me after explanation the Apostle had given of a conversation the two of us had one day. We were in the car when we were talking about the building in Amsterdam, where the services are held. We talked about the usage of the building, collaboration with other churches that follow Jesus and we talked about financing options for construction of an own building. My input as part of the conversation was that for starting with the construction of a building, all financial information, including budgets, a three to five year forecasts and such kind of information must be in order. The Apostle agreed with me that indeed that kind of information had to be readily available. Can you expect a technician whom had been anointed as Apostle to be able to set up that kind of information? Had he been anointed and blessed for that too? The answer is no. The word of Adonai clearly tells us that He had spread abilities and knowledge among humans (1 Corinthians 12:4-10), so we must work together for all the wisdom that is available on this world be used to its maximum potential and for the right reasons. The day that the Apostle had told the congregation about our conversation in the car and he had illustrated that God had been talking to me while we were in the car; I had realized my purpose for returning to The Netherlands. Was there no one else in The Netherlands that would have been able to do the job? Yes, there are but they are not called to perform the work for this specific Messianic Community. Should I have not obeyed and had not followed the path that Adonai had created for me, because believe it or not when in the house of Adonai, you still have your free will, Adonai would have aborted me for this mission and choose another for the work. The house would not have stayed in despair.

Adonai is showing me a path where the knowledge and wisdom that He has provided us, the highly educated, with is to be used for the construction and further professionalization of His houses around the world. This is a task for those that have been blessed with knowledge and wisdom. I truly believe that all the congregations that follow Jesus, whether they use the name church, congregation or Messianic Community, can use the help and input of highly educated persons.

Adonai, where are we heading? What exactly have you called us for? These are some of the questions that nowadays go through my mind. Five years ago I was happy if I had visited a church service once a month or every two weeks. Now I cannot live without the Holy Presence. Once you experience Adonai in spirit and in truth, your life will change. What used to be important, is not important anymore. It may sound strange, still that is my reality. There is a higher calling than working more than forty hours a week, earning a good salary, riding the coolest cars and wearing the latest models. Your soul and your spirit must be nourished too. The role that the highly educated can and must fulfill in the house of Adonai will be discussed in the next chapter.

CHAPTER 5

Talents that you have

5.1 Introduction

In the previous chapter you read how the Holy Spirit had been working in and through my life. For you, a highly educated person, it might be difficult to accept that you can have the same or even better experiences than what I had described with the Holy Spirit. Despite of all the reasons you may think that would make it impossible, I can tell you that it is possible. If someone would have told me, a year or even a day before everything that had happened, what I should be expecting, I would not have believed it. So I understand your doubts. In this chapter I want to take you on a quick tour through some basic information on the gifts, assets according to the scriptures that we all possess. I am sure that while reading you will notice how God has already been working in your life. For more in depth information on the topics you will read in this chapter, I refer to the books written by servants of God that discuss and provides enlightening on these topics.

5.2 Two sets of leader

Before getting into the gifts, I want to draw your attention on the kind of leaders, as described in the bible and the link to the role of highly educated people in the society. When you read the stories in the bible you will notice that there have been always two sets of leaders. The spiritual leader and the natural leader, both are tasks that require a lot of dedication, effort and skills. This division is still noticeable in our society today except that the relationship between the two sets of leaders is loose. David was, according to the scriptures, a great king and a servant of God. He had been one of the few natural leaders in the Old Testament who had a direct relationship with God. In Acts 13:22, you can read where it is stated that God had called him a man to His heart. Although King David had a direct relationship with God, God used Prophet Nathan to communicate with him. When David failed to listen to the voice of God, the man of God was there to take him back on track. That is why David had a close relationship with Apostle Nathan, a spiritual leader at that point in time. The scripture in 2 Samuel 7 clearly illustrates the aforementioned. What can we learn from this story? By means of the Holy Spirit, we, natural leaders and the public in general, can all have a direct contact with the God almighty, with Adonai, and yet the spiritual leaders are the ones to whom the plans of God are revealed.

The skills needed to fulfill one of the two leadership tasks, can only be provided by the Most High. Your skills can be cut, molded and polished throughout courses, experiences or study. But for this to happen, the skills must have been deposited in you. The highly educated is very often a supervisor, a manager, a director, or a business owner. In summary a natural leader. Where did all your skills come from? Are you a leader that listens to the voice of Adonai? Do you want to make a change for the better? If you are failing to listen to the voice of Adonai, whom is there to help you on track?

The natural leaders today are so busy with the quantity and quality of information that they receive that the time to listen to the voice of Adonai has vanished. There is so much to do that the time for communion with the Holy Spirit is simply forgotten. The business might not go as well as it used in the past. The customers are leaving or costs are increasing. There are a lot of circumstances and situations in the professional life for which we are looking for the answers. Where do we find all the answers? Maybe in new models or structures that will come forth from new ideas, but how do you come up with these? What is the driving force for new plans? Adonai has equipped the highly educated with several gifts. For the use of those gifts in all of their strength, a communion with the Holy Spirit is vital.

5.3 The Gifts of the Father

Paulus had said in his first letter to Peter: "*Each of you should use whatever gift you have received to serve others, as faithful stewards of God's grace in its various forms*". (1 Peter 4:10). These words do count nowadays for us, the highly educated, too. The Almighty has given you talents, not for you to keep them safe, but to use them wisely. In 1 Corinthians 12 we read in verse four to seven: "*There are different kinds of gifts, but the same Spirit distributes them. There are different kinds of service, but the same Lord. There are different kinds of working, but in all of them and in everyone it is the same God at work. Now to each one the manifestation of the Spirit is given for the common good*". The aforementioned text illustrates that there are three types of gifts being[13]:

Table 1 Type of Gifts

Source of the gifts	Category of gifts	Reference in the Bible
Gifts of the Father	Motivation	Romans 12:6-8
Gifts of the Son	Ministry	Ephesians 4:11
		1 Corinthians 12:28
Gifts of the Holy Spirit	Manifestation	1 Corinthians 12:7-11

Source: www.christcenteredmall.com/teachings/gifts

We will take a further look at the gifts that is provided by the Father which are the gifts that we all had received one or more in different measures.

The Almighty wants for you and me to understand the gifts that we had been blessed with. Each and every gift had been designed to help the body of Christ, for the body of Christ consists of several parts just like the human body[14]. To understand the motivational gifts, we must know their names and their meaning. "*For just as each of us has one body with many members, and these members do not all have the same function, so in Christ we, though many, form one body, and each member belongs to all the others. We have different gifts, according to the grace given to each of us. If your gift is prophesying, then prophesy in accordance with your faith; if it is serving, then serve; if it is teaching, then teach; if it is to encourage, then give encouragement; if it is giving, then give generously; if it is to lead, do it diligently; if it is to show mercy, do it cheerfully."* (Romans 12:4–8). These seven motivational gifts are further illustrated in the table below.

Table 2 The motivational gifts

Gift name	Meaning	Other names or titles	Some references in the Bible
Exhortation	Call one aside to encourage him.	Animator, Helper, Builder of Persons, Counselor, Optimistic	Proverbs 1:8, Acts 13:15 Philippians 4:4 Hebrews 13:1, 22
Giving	Giving, sharing offer or provide	Finance Manager, Finance Delegate, Volunteer, Supporter, Great faith in tithes.	Lucas 3:11 Romans 1:11; 11:28 Ephesians 4:28 1 Thessalonians 2:8
Leading (also referred to as gift of Administration)	To lead, to preside, to maintain, to practice, always ahead.	Director, Leader, Organizer, Pioneer, Supervisor, Visionary	Romans 12:8; 1 Thessalonians 5:12, 17 Tito 3:8, 14
Mercy	Having compassion, pain, receives and obtains mercy, sore about something to someone	Comforter, Counselor, Helper, Merciful Compassionate Peacemaker	Matthew 5:7, 9:27 Mark 5:19, 10:47, 48 Romans 9:15 Philippians 2:27

Prophecy	A talkative inspired	He who speaks, Prophet, Teacher, Inspirational Speaker	Matthew 13:14 Romans 12:6 1 Corinthians 12:10 2 Peter 1:20 Revelation 1:3
Service	Being serviced or minister, the office of deacon, support	Servant, Volunteer, Terminator, Benevolent, Worker, Follower.	Romans 15:25 2 Corinthians 8:4, 9:12 Revelation 2:19
Teaching	Who instructs and gives teaching	Researcher, Instructor Good Communicator, Trainer, Presenter.	John 3:2 Acts 1:1, 2:42, 4:2 1 Timothy 2:7

Source: www.dones.indubiblia.org

While I was searching for information for the completion of this chapter, God had led me to a website that contains a sermon of a servant of God that explains the way these gifts operate in our lives in a clear, familiar and simple manner[15]. The servant of God used the example of a family reunion where one person had just dropped the dessert on the floor. The example is derived from the weblog of God's servant Bill Gothard[16]. The servant explained that the reactions of the persons present, in accordance with the motivational gift that is operating thru each of them, would have been as follows:

Table 3 Reactions based on motivational gifts

Exhortation	Giving	Administration	Mercy
Next time, let us serve the dessert with the meal.	*I will be happy to buy a new dessert.*	*Jim, would you get the mop? Sue, please help pick it up and Mary, help me fix another dessert.*	*Don't feel badly. It could have happened to anyone.*

Prophecy	Serving	Teaching	
That is what happens when you are not careful.	*Oh, let me help you clean it up.*	*The reason that it fell is that it was too heavy on one side.*	

Source: http://cutr.org/sermon_notes/122610.pdf

This example is a situation that could happen every day and within each and every family. I do not know about you, but the reactions as illustrated in this example made a bell ring in my head. I was able to recognize the strength in the persons around me. What I had once considered as a weakness or an irritating reaction, is now a blessing. The point is, as we hear and learn in all the soft skills trainings, to use the best a person has at its maximum but in order to do so, you must understand the qualities a person has first. This does count also for you as a person.

This servant of God further explained, by means of summarizing information derived from the website of Institute for Basic Life Principles[17] and books of Mrs. Marilyn Hickey on motivational gifts, that the presence of these seven gifts in the congregation would lead to the emphasis and topics as illustrated in table 4.

Table 4 Place of the motivational gifts within the congregation

Exhortation	Giving	Administration	Mercy
Personal counseling and encouragement for every member to assist them in applying scriptural principles to their daily living.	*Generous programs of financial assistance to missionaries and other ministries.*	*Smooth-well running organization throughout the church so that every phase will be carried out decently and in order.*	*Special outreach and concern for the precise and varying feelings of individuals with a readiness to meet their needs.*

Prophecy	Serving	Teaching	
Well-prepared sermons exposing sin, proclaiming righteousness, and warning of judgment to come.	*Practical assistance to every member of the church to encourage them and to help them fulfill their responsibilities.*	*In-depth Bible studies with special emphasis on the precise meaning of words.*	

Source: http://cutr.org/sermon_notes/122610.pdf

As this example illustrates, though the basis for what has to be done in the congregation is the word of God, He wants that you, a blessed person, to help your neighbor with the earthly things for not all have the gift of prophecy. Get to know the blessings, the qualities God has given you and use them to the maximum potential to give Him glory and all the honor that He deserves for He has promised us via Prophet Joel that *"And everyone who calls on the name of the Lord will be saved; for on Mount Zion and in Jerusalem there will be deliverance, as the Lord has said, even among the survivors whom the Lord calls"*. (Joel 2: 32)

CONCLUSION

In the introduction, I posted the questions: Where did all the wisdom of all the developers of all the theories that we know nowadays come from? Where does your own wisdom come from? Inheritance of soft skills? If so, where did your parents or grandparents get their wisdom from? Have you considered that all of the knowledge and wisdom in your family is a blessing? Ever wondered what the purpose of such a blessing within your family is? What was your answer to these questions when you read them as part of the introduction and what is your answer now?

As I had explained in chapter one and two, I had lived the life that is so common for a person that was born in a family in the middle and/or upper class level. I grew up, studied and worked just the way that a highly educated person, that maybe you, did so in fact I am not that different from you or other highly educated people. I was able to live apart from my husband for nearly four years while experiencing the love and grace of God for my home and my family. Scripture, in 1 Corinthians 7: 5 became reality in our lives, for if it had not been that I had moved and separated from my husband, I do not know if I would have been serving God as I am doing today. Do not misunderstand me. My husband has never withheld me from adoring and worshipping God. On the contrary, he encourages me despite the fact that he does not attend the services with me. The point is, if I had not been on the island in the years that I had been there, I would not have been in contact with the Messianic Community that I am part of today. Now I know that Adonai, God Almighty of whom is written in the bible and so many books have been written about, indeed lives and He is a caring and loving father for all of us. In trials and tribulations,

He is at your side. In chapter three and four, I explained how I got the chance to experience the miracles, signs and wonders that can only be performed through the manifestations of the Holy Spirit. Do not let this be just informative, but search for an experience with the Holy Spirit so you can confirm for yourself all that I have written about the Holy Spirit.

In chapter five you read how you can unlock the potential God has put in you. You, too, can be an ambassador of the Most High. As Adonai has prepared me, He has also been preparing you to work for his ministry. Do not withstand your calling. In the appendix, I have included a small selection of scripture for you to read and meditate on. I strongly advise you to start reading the Bible, in order to get a better understanding of what God, Adonai, is expecting from you. The key is to obey God's word even in the circumstances where it seems like impossible. For it is in that situation, He shall show you His greatness and His mercy. Your faith in God is your greatest asset. Do cherish it.

> "I am saying this for your own good, not to restrict you,
> but that you may live in a right way in undivided devotion to the Lord."
> 1 Corinthians 7: 35

APPENDIX 1

Contact details

For queries and additional information you can contact the author at highly_favored@outlook.com

Please find below also the contact details for the congregation *Rains of Blessings for All Nations Messianic Community*
Rains of Blessings for All Nations Messianic Community – Curaçao, Dutch Caribbean
Apostle Orlando Balentina and Prophet Xiomara Balentina
Messianic Temple located at Van Kingsberglaan z/n, Curaçao, Dutch Caribbean
E-mail: yemayahs@yahoo.com

Rains of Blessings for All Nations Messianic Community – Amsterdam, The Netherlands
Apostle Claytis Balentina and Prophet Marvis Balentina
E-mail: suniva22@hotmail.com

Rains of Blessings for All Nations Messianic Community – Tilburg, The Netherlands
Apostle Omar Martha and Prophet Cidinha Martha
E-mail: omarmartha@hotmail.com

APPENDIX 2

More food for thought

In this section I present to you a small selection of scriptures from the Bible (*New International Version*) that speaks about knowledge and wisdom for you to read and meditate on.

Psalm 49
For the director of music. Of the Sons of Korah. A psalm.

[1] Hear this, all you peoples; listen, all who live in this world, [2] both low and high, rich and poor alike: [3] My mouth will speak words of wisdom; the meditation of my heart will give you understanding. [4] I will turn my ear to a proverb; with the harp I will expound my riddle: [5] Why should I fear when evil days come, when wicked deceivers surround me— [6] those who trust in their wealth and boast of their great riches? [7] No one can redeem the life of another or give to God a ransom for them— [8] the ransom for a life is costly, no payment is ever enough— [9] so that they should live on forever and not see decay. [10] For all can see that the wise die, that the foolish and the senseless also perish, leaving their wealth to others. [11] Their tombs will remain their houses forever, their dwellings for endless generations, though they had named lands after themselves. [12] People, despite their wealth, do not endure; they are like the beasts that perish. [13] This is the fate of those who trust in themselves, and of their followers,

who approve their sayings. [14] They are like sheep and are destined to die; death will be their shepherd (but the upright will prevail over them in the morning). Their forms will decay in the grave, far from their princely mansions. [15] But God will redeem me from the realm of the dead; he will surely take me to himself. [16] Do not be overawed when others grow rich, when the splendor of their houses increases; [17] for they will take nothing with them when they die, their splendor will not descend with them. [18] Though while they live they count themselves blessed—and people praise you when you prosper— [19] they will join those who have gone before them, who will never again see the light of life. [20] People who have wealth but lack understanding are like the beasts that perish.

Psalm 112

[1] Praise the LORD. Blessed are those who fear the LORD, who find great delight in his commands. [2] Their children will be mighty in the land; the generation of the upright will be blessed. [3] Wealth and riches are in their houses, and their righteousness endures forever. [4] Even in darkness light dawns for the upright, for those who are gracious and compassionate and righteous. [5] Good will come to those who are generous and lend freely, who conduct their affairs with justice. [6] Surely the righteous will never be shaken; they will be remembered forever. [7] They will have no fear of bad news; their hearts are steadfast, trusting in the LORD. [8] Their hearts are secure, they will have no fear; in the end they will look in triumph on their foes. [9] They have freely scattered their gifts to the poor, their righteousness endures forever; their horn will be lifted high in honor. [10] The wicked will see and be vexed, they will gnash their teeth and waste away; the longings of the wicked will come to nothing.

Proverbs 27: 23-27

Be sure you know the condition of your flocks, give careful attention to your herds; 24 for riches do not endure forever, and a crown is not secure for all generations. 25 When the hay is removed and new growth appears and the grass from the hills is gathered in, 26 the lambs will provide you with clothing, and the goats with the price of a field. 27 You will have plenty of goats' milk to feed your family and to nourish your female servants.

1 Corinthians 1: 18-25

18 For the message of the cross is foolishness to those who are perishing, but to us who are being saved it is the power of God. 19 For it is written: "I will destroy the wisdom of the wise; the intelligence of the intelligent I will frustrate." 20 Where is the wise person? Where is the teacher of the law? Where is the philosopher of this age? Has not God made foolish the wisdom of the world? 21 For since in the wisdom of God the world through its wisdom did not know him, God was pleased through the foolishness of what was preached to save those who believe. 22 Jews demand signs and Greeks look for wisdom, 23 but we preach Christ crucified: a stumbling block to Jews and foolishness to Gentiles, 24 but to those whom God has called, both Jews and Greeks, Christ the power of God and the wisdom of God. 25 For the foolishness of God is wiser than human wisdom, and the weakness of God is stronger than human strength.

2 Peter 1: 3 – 11

3 His divine power has given us everything we need for a godly life through our knowledge of him who called us by his own glory and goodness. 4 Through these he has given us his very great and precious promises, so that through them you may participate in the divine nature, having escaped the corruption in the world caused by evil desires. 5 For this very reason, make every effort to add to your faith goodness; and to goodness, knowledge; 6 and to knowledge, self-control; and to self-control, perseverance; and to perseverance, godliness; 7 and to godliness, mutual affection; and to mutual affection, love. 8 For if you possess these qualities in increasing measure, they will keep you from being ineffective and unproductive in your knowledge of our Lord Jesus Christ. 9 But whoever does not have them is nearsighted and

blind, forgetting that they have been cleansed from their past sins. [10] Therefore, my brothers and sisters, make every effort to confirm your calling and election. For if you do these things, you will never stumble, [11] and you will receive a rich welcome into the eternal kingdom of our Lord and Savior Jesus Christ.

ENDNOTES AND REFERENCES

1   OECD (2014) *EAG Glossary* Retrieved from http://www.oecd.org/ edu/EAG%20Glossary.pdf

2   OECD (2014) *Education at a Glance 2014: OECD Indicators*, OECD Publishing Retrieved from http:// dx.doi.org/10.1787/eag-2014-en

3   Ruben Hernandez (2000) *Herido pero aun Caminando* Retrieved from http://rubenh.com/?page_id=76

4   The Historical Research Center (1996) Inc. Keychain product of *Is Your Name here?*

5   Diamond Source of Virginia, Inc *(n.d.). Diamonds Education: What is a diamond?* Retrieved from http:// www.diamondsourceva.com/ Education/diamonds-what-is-a-diamond.asp

6   Diamond Source of Virginia, Inc *(n.d.) Heading: Diamonds Education: Diamond Cutting* Retrieved from http://www.diamondsourceva. com/Education/diamonds-diamond-cutting.asp

7   Hinn, B. [BringBackTheCross] *Road map into God's Presence part 1 and 2*, Fire Conference Lindenwold New Yersey, 19 November 2010 Retrieved from http://youtu.be/DAvXEqYlhrY and http://youtu.be/ Jhh3MT1j220

8   Hinn, B. (2004) *Good Morning Holy Spirit*, Thomas Nelson Inc., March 2004

9   OECD (2013), PISA 2012 *Assessment and Analytical Framework: Mathematics, Reading, Science, Problem Solving and Financial Literacy*, PISA, OECD Publishing. Retrieved from http://dx.doi. org/10.1787/9789264190511-en

10 Omar Alfanno (1994). *Así es la Vida,* [Recorded by Luis Enrique] On Luis Enrique [Medium of recording: CD Sony U.S. Latin, released on August 19, 1994].

11 Chosen People Ministries (n.d.) *Messianic Congregations,* Retrieved from http://www.chosenpeople.com/main/ index.php/ messianic-congregations-sp

12 Chosen People Ministries *(n.d.) Messianic Congregations FAQ,* Retrieved from http://www.chosenpeople.com/ main/index.php/ messianic-congregations-sp/messianic-congregations-faq

13 David Holt Boshart Jr. (1999) *Gifts of the Holy Spirit,* Retrieved from http://www.christcenteredmall.com/teachings/gifts

14 Herman Puchi *(n.d.) Los Dones Espirituales,* Retrieved from http:// www.dones.indubiblia.org

15 Church Upon the Rock (2010) *Seven Motivational Gifs* http://cutr. org/sermon_notes/122610.pdf

16 Gothard, B. (2008) *Spiritual Gifts pt15: Pinpointing Your Gift* Retrieved from http://lifeinconflict.blogspot.nl/2008/12/spiritual-gifts-pt15-pinpointing-your.html

17 Institute of Basic Life Princiles (n.d.) *What are the seven motivational gifts?* Retrieved from http://iblp.org/questions/ what-are-seven-motivational-gifts

ABOUT THE AUTHOR

Eunice was born and educated on the island of Curaçao in the Caribbean Sea. Eunice was born and educated on the island of Curaçao in the Caribbean Sea. She has a Master Degree in Accounting, and is certified as a Dutch Public Accountant. She has over 12 years of experience as a financial professional. In 2010 she had an encounter with The Holy Spirit that changed her view of life. This would turn out to be the first of many more experiences with the Holy Spirit that Jesus had send to us as our comforter. As rational as she was, she had to admit that God Almighty is more than a name written in Scripture. This view change was led, not by what people had told her or on what she had seen, but on what she had experienced on several occasions.

Currently Eunice lives in The Netherlands with her husband and their two children. She is active as a leader in the Rains of Blessings for All Nations Messianic Community.